PROVEN
HOLISTIC
TREATMENT

—— for ——

addiction

& chronic relapse

John J. Giordano C.A.P.

TATE PUBLISHING & *Enterprises*

This book is designed to provide accurate and authoritative
information with regard to the subject matter covered. This
information is given with the understanding that neither the
author nor Tate Publishing, LLC is engaged in rendering legal,
professional advice. Since the details of your situation are fact
dependent, you should additionally seek the services of a com-
petent professional.

ISBN: 1–5988637–5-4

PROVEN HOLISTIC TREATMENT

_____ for _____

addiction

& chronic relapse

Dedication

Dedicated to those cold and angry lost souls, who know neither success nor failure, who stand along life's highways watching their lives go by, becoming "the effect rather than the cause," blaming everyone else for their misfortunes. May GOD rescue them from this hell on earth and awaken them to the path of enlightenment!

Acknowledgments

I would like to thank all of my contributors, especially my wife Michele, for their patience and support. Allene Poulk and Dorothy Rodwell, thank you so much for all your help. To Zena and Rex Lyons for all their assistance in making this manual a reality. To my partners and friends, who shared their experience, strength, and hope, which made this book possible. To the editorial and production staff at Tate Publishing, and in particular Mark Mingle, for all their help, and to all addicts who have lived and died so that this knowledge could be made available.

Table of Contents

Foreword

This book is an important tool for those seeking to recover from the abuse of numerous substances. It is written in a manner that speaks (not preaches) to all, no matter their background or addiction. Its intent is not to confuse or alienate a group, but to appeal to a wide range of people. This book reads in a familiar tone, as though a friend is talking to you. It is not filled with complicated or sophisticated language, so that everyone will gain the fullest understanding of the text. I think John Giordano has been successful in creating a work that will be used and appreciated by all those who read it.

Fritz Jean
Director New Talent
Printing, Miami, Florida

Preface

A recovering addict wrote the words on these pages. This information is an accumulation of years of successful, continued abstinence from drugs and alcohol. The knowledge was passed down to me by a number of addicts/alcoholics who have long-term clean time/sobriety and who continually work on their bad character habits. In these pages, you will find some of the excuses addicts use so that they do not have to change. You will also find the antidote for those excuses, learn how to overcome them, and move forward. Some pages suggest that you do some writing or exercise. Please don't take these lightly; they definitely help more than you know. Do the work, create the change, and enjoy your recovery.

About the Author

John Giordano is a recovered addict who used and abused drugs, alcohol, and anything else that felt good. He was born and raised in New York City, South Bronx, and Harlem. Mr. Giordano was in different ethnic gangs: Black, Hispanic, Irish, and Italian, from the age of 11 to 14.

He then joined a Karate school and left the gangs behind. By the age of 17, he was already the youngest to ever hold the rank of black belt; this was during the days when karate was studied by very few, as compared to today. During this time he also quit school—in the beginning of the ninth grade—and went to work as an apprentice brick-layer. After he became the United States Karate champion at the age of 17, he moved to Florida.

When he arrived in Florida, little did he know that he would begin a journey that almost cost him his life! He started experimenting with drugs and became like two people. One person was a kind and considerate human being, and the other was a self-centered, self-absorbed person who was not able to take responsibility for his own actions. He owned his own business, had a family, dealt drugs, and collected money for the smugglers.

Along with becoming a legend in the Martial Arts, he led two lives. Eventually they began to merge. Luckily, his friends and family did an intervention on him and he went to treatment. But he didn't go to get well; he just went to get everyone off his back. Something happened while he was in treatment: some call it a spiritual awakening.

Today John has his G.E.D. and went back to school for addiction training. He has received his C.A.P. (Certified Addiction Professional), M.A.C. (Master Addiction Counselor) and a master's certification in Neuro-Linguistic Programming. He is also certified in Hypnotherapy and EMDR. Two years into recovery, John raised some money, put a treatment team together, and opened up his first treatment center, which was called "New Life."

Today, John continues to design drug treatment programs and owns and operates a unique holistic treatment program that specializes in chronic relapse. He designed this treatment program to deal with the whole person: mind, body, and spirit. His detoxification, outpatient, inpatient, and long-term treatment program utilizes cutting-edge technologies of the 21st century. John now teaches at the Addiction Training Institute, teaching other people how to treat addiction.

John has never relapsed and has had continuous freedom from drugs, alcohol, and many unhealthy behaviors for the last 21 years. Recovery was not easy for John. He suffered many consequences. Watching his children go through the pains of addiction was especially painful. He knows the feelings of helplessness that family members feel and the guilt that goes along with it. Thank God, today his family is intact and doing well. John's life has changed beyond his wildest dreams. This book is John's way of giving back to those of us who struggle with this insidious disease. May God continue to bless us all!

John Giordano is a recovering addict who celebrates 21 years of continuous recovery. He has received numerous certifications in addiction treatment, such as C.A.P., M.A.C. & C.C.J.S. John is also a part owner/program director of the Holistic Addiction Treatment Program in North Miami Beach, Florida. He has been the recipient of many distinguished awards, such as the Martin Luther King Award, and the Homeless Humanitarian Award. John is also in the Black Belt Hall of Fame as a result of his many accomplishments and contributions to the martial arts, including becoming a 100 black belt and a national karate champion. He is also the author of the book *Proven Holistic Treatment for Addicts with a History of Chronic Relapse,* and was previously the host of a one-hour call in television talk show on addiction.

For more information, please contact John Giordano: c/o Giordano & Goldfarb's Holistic

Addiction Treatment Program 1590 N.E. 162nd St. • North Miami Beach, Fl 33162 • www.drugrehabcenter.com

MAY A HIGHER POWER CONTINUE
TO BLESS US ALL.

WITH LOVE AND GRATITUDE

JOHN J. GIORDANO
"A GRATEFUL RECOVERING
ADDICT"

Holistic Addiction Treatment for the 21st Century

About Addiction

A number of factors contribute to the development of addictive behaviors, such as early childhood trauma, mental disorders, family history, and environment.

Early childhood trauma includes sexual and/or physical abuse, neglect, or abandonment. Some of the mental illnesses that often accompany addiction are learning disabilities, attention deficit disorder, bipolar disorder, anxiety disorders, depression, and a multitude of others.

Addictions are often developed through an attempt to alleviate the symptoms of these illnesses. The 2001 NHSDA report states that among adults with mental illness in 2001, 20.3% (about 3 million people) were dependent on or abused alcohol or illicit drugs. The rate among adults without serious mental illnesses was about 6%.

Family History is also very important as certain genetic factors that are attributed to behavior may be passed down from generation to generation. Genetics is also further influenced by the physical environment surrounding the individual. Some people develop their addictions at an early age and never learn to cope with adversity, thereby propagating their addictive behavior. As these individuals grow older, these behaviors become more deeply rooted, and their addiction grows stronger until it becomes more difficult to satisfy.

Addiction destroys a human being on every level of their existence. It damages them mentally, emotionally, physically, and spiritually, leaving them virtually drowning in a sea of loneliness and despair. The hope that they may one day win their battle to stop using vanishes completely. They lose touch with their Higher Power and their life becomes a seemingly endless series of failures that eventually leads to total yielding to their addiction and their pain. People suffering from addiction not only abuse drugs and alcohol, but every person, place, and thing with whom they come in contact. Although it is not their intention to cause such tumultuous pain in those around them, these battered emotions seep into all areas of their lives, making attempts at recovery futile.

The Holistic Approach
(Detox & Treatment)

In years past, addiction treatment centers have focused primarily on treating the psychological aspects of the disease of addiction, while neglecting to address the delicate inter-connective balance of the body, mind and spirit. Most individuals who enter into a 28-day treatment program receive education about their addiction that only scratches the surface of the underlying issues of their addictive behavior and are introduced to the program of AA (Alcoholics Anonymous), NA (Narcotics Anonymous), and GA (Gamblers Anonymous). After treatment, clients are encouraged to live in a supportive environment such as a 3/4 way house. However, most return to their homes unprepared to live a life without drugs. In some cases, this traditional approach to treatment may be effective. Usually, the success rate of traditional addiction treatment is very low.

The wisdom of Western Medicine is that if you have a symptom, treat it. If a person has a headache, they take Ibuprofen or Acetaminophen to alleviate the symptoms. But they never determine the root cause of the headache. The Holistic approach to medicine and treatment holds that human beings have a body, a mind, and a spirit. These elements of the human being are intertwined and exist in a delicate balance that determines positive or negative physical/mental health. The holistic method respects this balance and approaches treatment with the understanding that in order to achieve positive results, this equilibrium must be restored.

An exciting new detox treatment that deals primarily with painless detox from drugs and alcohol, known as Ibogaine, has experienced particular success in the holistic approach to treatment. This treatment is used for the detox of alcohol opiates, Heroin and Methadone. Typically, it takes about seven days to three months in order to detox an individual who is addicted to Heroin or Methadone; detox treatment with Ibogaine lasts between 24–36 hours, with little to no side effects.

Ibogaine is a rain forest alkaloid derived from the root of the Tabernanthe iboga (Apocynacea family), which is a shrub indigenous to West Central Africa. Ibogaine is used by the native people in low doses to relieve fatigue, hunger, and thirst. The pharmacogenic effects of Ibogaine have been researched for over 100 years. The anti-addictive properties of Ibogaine were first reported in 1982.

People who are substance-dependent have stated that Ibogaine treatment puts them into a waking dream state. These Ibogaine-induced dreams are usually centered on early childhood traumas and other important developmental events that occurred during turning points in their life. Once awakened from these dream-like visions, insight into interpreting the root causes of their addictive personalities are often revealed. At the end of the Ibogaine treatment, opiate, alcohol, and cocaine-dependent individuals experienced some relief or the total cessation of the drug or alcohol craving. Also, opiate-dependent clients stated that their opiate withdrawal symptoms were alleviated.

Dr. Deborah Mash from the University of Miami, funded under NIDA (National Institute of Drug Addiction), is a Neuro Scientist and Chief researcher of the Ibogaine Project. Dr. Mash has been in collaboration with me, John Giordano, for the last ten years to create a new holistic treatment approach to addiction that is more effective than current methodologies. This alliance formed against drug abuse encompasses Ibogaine treatment along with other modalities that work cooperatively to restore healthy body, mind, and spirit functioning.

Body

The 21st century holistic approach begins first with the body. What we ingest internally creates the foundation for the proper functioning of our mind and body. Stimulants and toxins such as caffeine, refined sugars, processed foods, food additives, and a poor overall diet contribute immensely to an imbalance in brain chemistry. It is crucial that these foods and additives be eliminated or significantly reduced in the diet in order to restore healthy brain functioning. In exchange, a complete diet consisting of fruit, fiber, fish, turkey, whole grains, protein, and lots of water must be embraced.

Generally, those entering treatment are dehydrated, hypo/hyperglycemic, and protein deficient. They also need to be evaluated for certain bacterial and fungal infections, such as Candida albicans. Chemical dependency along with an insufficient diet can wreak havoc on an individual's delicate immune system. These complications can contribute to depression, agitation, decreased energy stores, and eventually, to relapse.

Along with a proper diet, a good vitamin supplement regimen is also necessary because much of the vitamin, mineral, and amino acid stores, which are the building blocks of neurotransmitters in the brain, are depleted from drug and alcohol abuse. Also, exercise, meditation, neuro-feedback, and stress reduction techniques are essential in keeping the mind and body stable. Some excellent disciplines for achieving mind/body congruency are yoga, tai chi, and karate.

Acupuncture is a modality that can often assist the body in the rebalancing process. This treatment allows energy to flow into the body to stimulate the production of neurotransmitters and calm some of the cravings for drugs and alcohol. Also, nurturing the body with hot baths and steams, good music, and gentle relaxation will help to rid the body of toxins and restore peace of mind.

Mind

Current research has suggested that certain chemical imbalances in the brain appear to play an important role in contributing to addiction. The use and abuse of drugs and alcohol causes brain chemistry to deviate even further from the normal range. The 2001 NHSDA reported that those who use illicit drugs were twice as likely to have serious mental illnesses as compared with those adults who did not abuse illicit drugs. With chronic abuse, a vicious cycle is formed that grows exponentially over time. This causes a lack of concentration, emotional instability, feelings of depression, and a total absence of a moral and spiritual balance. In many cases, medication is necessary to correct the chemical imbalance resulting from mental illnesses. In some gamblers suffering from chronic relapse, for example, psychotropic medication is an integral part of their recovery. It is paramount to change the root causes of the addictive behavior in order for treatment to be successful. Some effective new therapies that can effectuate tremendous changes in behavior are EMDR, NLP, and neuro-feedback.

Eye Movement Desensitization and Reprocessing (EMDR) is an approach to psychotherapy that uses eye movements to stimulate the information processing in the brain. This therapy provides much faster results than traditional therapy. It is often used for treating trauma such as sexual abuse, domestic violence, war, crime, depression, addiction, phobias, and self-esteem issues. A recent study performed by Kaiser-Permanente found that EMDR was twice as effective as typical therapy. Overall, EMDR allows the brain to heal its own wounds at the same rate that the rest of the body is able to heal its physical ailments, making a long and tedious recovery a thing of the past.

Another interesting modality that is very effective is Neuro Linguistic Programming (NLP). NLP is the study of the structure of subjective experience. It is a therapeutic tool that can reprogram a client's belief systems and behaviors. NLP incorporates a set of models on how communication can be affected by subjective experience. It utilizes a change in language and thought processes to understand behaviors.

Neuro-feedback is a cutting-edge technique that trains the brain in order to help it improve body function regulation and overall brain health. When there is poor brain functioning, it is recognized through the EEG (Electroencephalogram). By challenging the brain, much like muscles are challenged in physical exercise to improve their strength, normal brain functionality can be restored. The benefits of neuro-feedback include developing healthier sleep patterns, obtaining relief from anxiety and depression, and enhanceing mental attention and emotional balance. Emotional management is very important in how an individual reacts to a particular situation.

Spirit

One of the most important steps in recovery is psychological awareness. Becoming aware of personal speech, thoughts, body language, and actions is crucial in maintaining a life free from chemical dependency. It is important to learn how to avoid the pitfalls of negative thoughts and negative people. An individual must learn that it is more important to be kind than to be right, and to develop values, integrity, and finally, to learn to be good to oneself and others by trusting in a Higher Power.

By believing in a Higher Power, it is easier to submit oneself to recovery and treatment. The relationship that is developed through spirituality enriches life and gives hope and inspiration. Recovering individuals discover that a life free from the clutches of drugs and alcohol is not only possible, but is a life well worth living. Spirituality is the foundation for the development of a positive living philosophy.

Twelve-step programs are a spiritual way of life. They are non-denominational, anonymous, and non-controversial. The success of these programs is based upon "the therapeutic value of one addict helping another." Many atheist and agnostic individuals have been able to embrace the twelve steps with their own personal concept of a Higher Power. The role of a Higher Power in their life becomes G.O.D. (Good Orderly Direction). Every addict that is serious about recovery is able to attain serenity and fullness of life by applying these steps and these principles to their daily life.

Conclusion

Addiction treatment has come a long way through the years and still has a long way to go.

In the 21st century, it appears that the most effective approach to treating addictive disorders is the holistic approach. In this approach, individuals suffering from the disease of addiction are treated with respect, dignity, and as a whole person with a body, mind and spirit. It takes time to heal and to restore the proper functioning of these three elements, and they are fundamental to a successful recovery.

It is very important to increase public awareness of addiction in order to decrease the stigma that surrounds it, which is preventing some of the afflicted from accessing necessary treatment. There are roughly 5 million people in this country who need addiction treatment that are not receiving it. If our communities embraced a more holistic attitude toward recovery, perhaps there would be a decrease in the number of people in need of treatment and an increase in resources available to the population suffering from addiction. Knowledge of addiction is a powerful tool that will assist our planet in defending itself against this moral, physical, and spiritual decay.

Here are some slogans that I hated … today, I live by them—how ironic!

Drugs are bad for you.
Give time, time, and be consistent.
It works if you work it, so work
it. You are worth it.
If you change your response, you
will change your outcome.
Nothing changes if nothing changes.
Life is what you make it.
Today is the first day of the rest of your new life.

Looking outside myself never gave me what I was looking for. Only when I looked inside did I find my Truth!!!

Part I

Therapy

Go to a therapist that is familiar with addiction and dual disorders. Having dual disorders means that both the disease of addiction and a possible mental disorder or chemical imbalance are present. Examples of these mental disorders or chemical imbalances are bipolar disorder, obsessive-compulsive disorder, attention deficit disorder, schizophrenia, and depression, among others.

Definitions of the most common mental disorders associated with addiction are available in the appendices at the back of this book followed by the glossary. Make sure the type of therapist that you go to helps you to build up your positive attributes and does not come from a shaming place. I suggest you find a therapist who knows addiction, who is trained in Neuro-Linguistic Programming, who knows Gestalt therapy, and who believes in a humanistic approach.

Psychiatric Evaluation

Get evaluated by a psychiatrist who knows addiction. Get a physical and check for Hyper or Hypoglycemia and Candida albicans infection, which can cause irritability, depression, and confused thinking. Don't be ashamed if the doctor asks you to be on medication. Most of us have a chemical imbalance and need to be evened out. Most addicts with chronic relapses have an underlying disorder that is quite often never addressed.

Recovering Strategy

Having a good recovery strategy starts with writing a list of things you feel you have to do. When you were drinking and drugging, you probably ignored your responsibilities; so look at each item on your list and prioritize them. What you may want to consider is chipping away at situations that you want to change, but keep recovery as your main goal.

Talk to your therapist, your sponsor, or any other person whom you respect and trust; make sure they understand addiction and let them help you with your decision-making. Keep in mind that your brain only seems to be working properly and that the person you are seeking guidance from needs to understand addiction in order to effectively help you. There is no shame in asking for help, so get rid of the excuses. Recovery comes before anything or anyone. If you put anyone or anything before your recovery, you are sure to use and lose—no recovery, no hope, and no life worth living.

Medication

If you need to be on medication, it may take from four to six weeks to stabilize. If you feel sluggish and out of sorts, call your doctor. Most often, it's your body adjusting to the medication. After four to six weeks, if you still don't feel right, speak to your doctor again. Everyone is different. Be patient; sometimes you may have to change your medication a few times. Don't get discouraged. If you need medication and don't take it, the alternative will be a never-ending story.

After you have been taking your medication and start feeling good, please don't stop or adjust your dosage. This is a very common mistake for people to make, and generally if they do, they relapse right after. If by any chance you consider this, call your doctor. If you are leery of taking medication, consider alternative medication. There are herbs that are used for relaxation, and there are herbs that will help with depression. Don't shortchange yourself. Give it a chance.

Learn to trust the professionals who are treating you. *Allow them to do their job.*

**I'm having difficulty finding my way.
I need to reach out for help. What
happened to my pink cloud?**

Vitamins

Vitamin therapy is extremely important. It has taken me years to develop a balanced combination that will help create a sense of well being and assist greatly in reducing cravings. Years of research by numerous laboratories suggest that these products may help to rebuild some of the damage caused by drugs and alcohol.

Recovery is an ongoing practice; it is not something we do for a little while. Our disease is a chronic progressive illness that can be arrested if we follow a recovery lifestyle. Always check with your doctor before taking these vitamins and herbs.

Now, here is the protocol we recommend:

Ultimate Cleanse, "Natures Choice"

Mental clarity formula helps rebuild neurotransmitters:

◊ 5HTP helps with sleep, cravings, and replenishing serotonin levels.

◊ Kudzu helps with urges to use alcohol.

◊ My Self Defense Multi Vitamin and Mineral Formula helps to rebuild the body.

◊   Nerve Factor, "Michael's" helps with mood swings.

◊   St. Johns Wort helps with mood swings and depression.

◊   Holistic Anti-Anxiety formula has a calming effect and reduces anxiety and helps with sleep.

◊   SAMe helps with depression.

I also have my own vitamin line, which I strongly recommend, described in detail at the back of the book.

Take detoxification formula for 90 days. Take "Nature's Choice" AM/PM formula for 6 to 12 months. Then get a more specific protocol from a licensed Nutritionist. More is not necessarily better. Take a soy [whey free] protein drink every morning. Most addicts are protein deficient. Use other herbs and vitamins as directed. Don't expect an immediate response. These are not drugs, but a way of helping rebuild what we have destroyed: our mind, body, and spirit.

Vitamins are supplements. They must be taken with food unless stated otherwise. Suggestion: every 30 to 45 days, stop all vitamins for three days; then begin again where you left off. This will help your body better utilize the vitamins. Amino acids are usually–taken on an empty stomach for best absorption.

To order any of the vitamins described above, call toll free 1–800–559–9503.

Diet

Diet is very important, especially early in the recovery process. Do your best not to eat white flour products such as bread, cakes, cookies, etc. Do your best not to eat dairy products such as cheese, milk, etc. Beware of caffeine products such as coffee, tea, and colas. Drink juice and plenty of water (about 3 quarts a day). Eat fruit and cereal in the morning, eat a lot of greens and a protein dishes (5 to 6 ounces of fish, chicken, tofu, etc.), and eat small portions of carbohydrates for dinner such as sweet potatoes, vegetables, grains, and nuts. Get proteins into your diet throughout the day such as fish, turkey, soybeans, etc., and do your best not to eat past 7 PM.

Eat 5 small meals a day. This will help to keep your energy level up and may help speed up your metabolism. Complex carbohydrates (baked potatoes, vegetables) are good forms of energy during the day, but not at night. When you are not eating well, food can help create a negative attitude. When you start to eat well you can produce a healthier outlook, feel good about yourself, see things positively, and slowly create change in yourself for the better.

Please don't beat yourself up if you happen

to fall back into old eating habits. Pick yourself up and start again. It takes time to change. How much time is strictly up to you, so stop feeling sorry for yourself. Get up and make it happen, because you can.

Exercise

Exercise can and will relieve stress. It is important to ask your doctor how often and how much is best for you. My suggestion, after medical clearance is given, is to walk at a moderate pace for 10 to 15 minutes a day. Then increase the duration slowly to 30–45 minutes a day. Swimming is a great way to get in shape. Again, begin slowly, a minimum of 5 to 10 minutes a day, 4–5 days a week; increase your pace and length of time slowly.

When working out, make sure your heartbeat is up and your breathing is hard, but not to the point that you're out of breath. Weight lifting is good when combined with an aerobic workout. I suggest karate, tai chi, tennis, basketball, or any activity that can hold your attention, because we tend to get bored very easily. Exercise releases stress, and it is very important to have a healthy outlet because when an addict becomes stressed, he/she reaches for his/her drug of choice. Stress equals using, and using equals destruction, pain, and suffering.

Meditation

I believe that this too shall pass. The alternative is jails, institutions, or death. This time I choose recovery.

Meditation is the key to the locked doorway of your subconscious mind. It will open it up and let you take a look at your unresolved issues. Meditate morning and night to center yourself. Here is an example: Sit with your back straight at the edge of a bed, or sit in a chair; breathe in slowly through your nose and slowly out of your mouth. While meditating, don't worry about being fidgety or about thoughts flying all around, just focus on your breathing and say to yourself, "In and out."

Imagine an open door on your right temple and one on your left. Then see your thoughts going in and going out and just focus on your breathing. Do this for at least five minutes everyday and every night. Slowly increase your meditation to thirty minutes; this is not a requirement, just a suggestion. It takes time, hard work, and especially patience, but the rewards outweigh the hard work ten to one. Don't forget, people all over the world have been using meditation for centuries.

Massage

For the first year, do your best to get at least one deep tissue massage a week. These massages will help in relieving emotional stress, which is trapped in the very fibers of your muscles. Our bodies get stressed, not just our minds. Learn to treat all three areas: body, mind, and spirit. Massage will help you to stay centered and relaxed. It is another way to get high: High on Life! If you don't have the money to get a professional massage, trade off with a friend.

Natural Detoxification

Using current "detox" methods, failure occurs much more often than not, and most people never make it to receive the type of treatment they need. This is because most of the individuals leaving detoxification centers are still drug affected, rendering them unable to make clear decisions about treatment programs and recovery options. In order to effectively combat this alarming and growing problem, alternative treatment methods must be explored. These should be used in conjunction with other therapies.

Proper diet and nutrition consisting of vitamin C, amino-acids, essential fatty acids, and proteins can have a very positive effect. Vitamin C is a very potent antioxidant and will help cleanse and destroy free radicals in the tissues. It also aids in releasing intestinal toxins, which are an important component of getting clean and sober.

I suggest taking 3000 mg of vitamin C every four hours for three to five days. Amino acids, especially glutamine, will stimulate the body's natural opiates and endorphins to help alleviate some cravings. Essential fatty acids, such as flax oil, in combination with foods containing proteins (cysteine of methionine)—such as yogurt, eggs, codfish, sesame paste, garlic, and onions—will allow fat soluble toxins to become water for excretion through sweat and urine.

In order to facilitate and expedite excretion of toxic substance, perspiration must be enhanced. This should be done through rigorous exercise and steam therapy, such as Turkish steam baths, saunas, or a hot whirlpool bath. Outdoor activities like beach outings are also good. Following heavy perspiration, the individual should clean themselves with a high-fat soap to remove toxins excreted on the surface of the skin and prevent their reabsorption.

Another area to consider when approaching detoxification from alcohol and drugs is the colon. The colon is a major part of the excretory system and is responsible for eliminating food and other body wastes, as well as protecting us from infection and disease. In a normally functioning colon, cleansing is achieved with the help of billions of friendly bacteria that make up some 70% of the dry weight of our fecal waste.

The delicate balance of this internal ecosystem can very easily be disturbed by factors including stress, pollution, poor food and drink choices, certain drugs, smoking and exposure to toxic substances. Therefore, I suggest a series of three colonics given in a one week period, beginning about the third or fourth day of detox treatment. These colonics will remove the wastes created by years of mistreating your body and will definitely aid in your intestine's ability to absorb nutrients. You only have one body, so it is time to stop treating it like you have a spare.

Acupuncture

Acupuncture is an ancient Chinese art of healing that works directly with your energy system (Chi). It assists your body in healing itself from disease. This is especially good for addicts. Acupuncture can help with urges and cause you to feel relaxed. It cannot hurt you, and you have more to gain than to lose. We believe that acupuncture will help rebuild your Neurotransmitters, those chemicals we deplete when we use drugs or alcohol.

Acupuncture is not a cure for addiction, but it definitely is a powerful piece of the recovery puzzle. Addicts are depleted of their vital energies, which is why they suck energy from everyone, especially from those who love them. Stop being a taker, and learn to be more of a giver. Heal your energy flow, and you will heal your soul.

Values/Principles

Create a list of the things you value. For example, I would list my recovery, spirituality, relationships, my job, my life, my body, honesty, open communication with others, etc. After creating this list of values, prioritize them in order of importance. Every day, take a look at your list and see if you compromised any of your values. If you did, look at what you compromised and ask yourself, "What do I need to do for myself to get my principles back in order?" and take action. Recognize and remember the difference between how you feel when you uphold your values and how you feel when you don't. Honor yourself and your values because if you don't, you will create low self-esteem and an environment to use and abuse. This leads to a life of misery and despair.

Journaling

Keep a journal. Buy a small wire note pad that fits in your shirt pocket, and write down your reactions to various situations and feelings that you may have experienced during the day. By reading your journal every night, you will start to see a pattern of how your thoughts caused you to react both positively and negatively. After a week, go back over your journal and start to alter the behaviors that you want to change. After doing this for a while, you will be amazed at how much progress you can make in changing your thought patterns and the way you respond to situations.

When we do drugs/alcohol, we lose touch with our true self. Journaling will help you to rid yourself of negative thoughts and learn another way of thinking and acting. This will be beneficial for you and the people around you. Recovery is about self-discovery and change.

Boredom

Each day, do your best to challenge yourself. Do something different for fun, do something relaxing, or do something you've never done before. When you're bored, it's because you're boring. Get up and participate in life; don't have contempt prior to investigation. If you feel lonely, don't stay alone; change where you are, get busy, call a friend, call your sponsor, go to a meeting, or help another recovering addict. Do something productive, and stop playing the victim. Deal with life, or life will deal with you. Addicts in general seem to always want some kind of action, some drama in their lives. The problem is that we mistake boredom for serenity and choose unhealthy ways to create excitement in our lives. When we invest our time wisely, we no longer mistake boredom for serenity.

Spirituality

Spirituality is not a religion. It can be a great refuge from pain and suffering. A Higher Power seems to be present in recovering people with long-term abstinence. All I can tell you is that if I had not come to an understanding of my spirituality I do not believe I could have stayed clean all these years. The choice is yours.

An example of spirituality is being kind instead of right. Do your best not to lie, cheat, or steal. Now don't expect perfection, just progress. No one is perfect, at least no one on this planet. If you really want to get high, you will get high, but if you really don't want to get high, get out of yourself and help another human being to help themselves. See what you can contribute instead of what you can take. You will be amazed at the results.

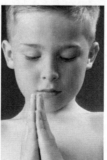

Addiction

Addiction is a behavior done continuously in spite of reoccurring adverse consequences. Addiction hides in a multitude of behaviors; gambling, spending, sex, relationships, work, exercise, and food are just a few examples. Moderation and sometimes abstinence is necessary. Stopping the drinking/drugging is only the first step in the recovery process. You must learn that when it comes to your addiction and your life becomes unmanageable, you are powerless.

If you are not consistent, nothing will ever change, unless you seek the proper help. Alone against your addiction, you are sure to lose, but together nothing can stop us. Don't reinvent the wheel; follow directions of people who are the winners, those who have maintained a life free of drugs and alcohol, and that includes any other behaviors that cause us to become out of balance. When we truly desire to work along spiritual lines, our highs and lows flow more easily and our need for living on the edge no longer becomes an obsession.

Work Addiction

Be careful of work addiction; it will get you every time. Yes, we must pay our bills; yes, we need to feed our families; yes, we have to pay back those debts; and yes, we owe it to our employer. But these are all the reasons that work addiction throws people off the path of recovery, and it is a sure relapse. Priorities start to change; you find other things becoming more important than your recovery, but at what price? Recovery is about balance; it is about first things first, and recovery is definitely first.

If you don't overcome your addiction, there is no job—which means no money. You will not be able to pay those bills or feed the family, so who are you trying to kid? How come you didn't care about it when you were drinking or drugging?

Yes, in the beginning things may not happen as fast as you would like, and you may lose some things, but anything is possible if you stay clean and sober. You have a disease of "I want it now," and "I want more." Recovery teaches us patience, tolerance, and gratitude for what we do have. I would like to think, "No pain, no gain."

In the beginning, start slowly; do not take on too many responsibilities at the same *time*. Do not work long hours. Early in recovery, do your best not to work more than 30 hours a week. Slow down and you will get much more accomplished. Life is a journey, not a race. Do this for a minimum of one year, and if nothing changes, we will gladly refund your misery.

Jobs

Now, let's talk about people who are able to get back all they lost and become successful in early recovery. Here is my take on it. Addicts who are capable of making lots of money quickly have trouble with honesty and humility. They get caught up in the frenzy of making money, and lo and behold, they are using again. Because they are resourceful and creative, money comes relatively easy. Addicts are addicted to quick money and easy pickings and are easily distracted from their primary purpose, which is to live along spiritual lines.

Rapid success can lead to rapid failure. Self-centeredness and self-importance will cause them to lose humility and willingness to change. Be careful of these pitfalls. There is a solution! We have to change our ways. Change is hard, but with the help of meetings, the steps, and a sponsor, we can do it. Stay grounded, work a program of honesty and humility, and don't take the easy way out. A good therapist should be used for these underlying issues. I believe in covering all my bases. If you want to be a winner, do the work. You will definitely get the job done.

I'm not like these people, I have plenty of money. I don't understand why they keep telling me I'm in denial.

Loneliness and Emptiness

Loneliness and emptiness are products of a lack of spirituality and low self-esteem. We all feel this way at one time or another. It just means that we are human. A way to remedy these feelings of despair is to create a gratitude list. If we open our eyes, we can see that we are never alone or empty when we allow others in, including our *Higher Power.* Get over the "poor me's" and enjoy whatever life you *do* have.

My life is too good…I will succeed.

You're NOT Alone

If you came from an alcoholic or drug using family, learn how it may have affected your personality and the way you deal or don't deal with life. I suggest you do some research on Adult Children of Alcoholics (ACOA). It doesn't matter whether it is drugs or alcohol; the results are all the same. I suggest you purchase a book called *Adult Children of Alcoholics Syndrome.* (See the bibliography). This may help you realize that there is hope in your life and that you are not alone. Each addiction has a specific set of symptoms, and all of them are interrelated. Some of the books I suggest you read are listed in the bibliography.

I don't want to relapse.

After reading this suggested literature, you should have a pretty good handle on what to do in order to live a full and rewarding life. Information is great, but without action it is meaningless. So begin your new life now. God knows you have earned it. Action begins by following directions—not your own. So what are you waiting for? Go for it! If I did it, so can you.

Change

In early recovery, everything may seem overwhelming, very difficult, and a like a lot of work. It will appear boring and repetitive, and your life will seem to be lonely and frustrating, but as long as you follow suggestions, these feelings will pass. Change is frightening, but as soon as you overcome your fears and look back, you'll realize that it wasn't such a big a deal.

Recovery is discovering who you are and who you can become. You can change your life to become all that our Creator intended us to be—loving, productive human beings. Don't be afraid to ask for help. Anyone who has maintained any length of time in recovery sought help and obviously got what they needed. The only thing you must change is everything. If you do not change, the only thing that will is your clean date. So give yourself some time—how much time is up to our Higher Power and us. Our life begins when we say it does. So say it.

Living in the Past and Future

People who are addicted tend to live and dwell in the past, often skipping over the present. This leads to recreating past fears in their future. I believe we do this to keep us feeling more remorse and more pain, so then we can go deeper into depression and then have an excuse to use a mood-altering substance.

By working the 12 steps of AA/NA/GA/OA, we can learn to live in the present and begin to realize that what we do in the present creates our future. This is how change works. Our past is from where we draw our experience. There are no failures, only lessons. So stop living in your past, because if you don't, you won't have a future worth living.

When we live in the future, we get overwhelmed; "I'm not going to get this," "I'm not going to have that," "I'm not going to be successful." Doing this, we miss the chance to change. Most things we wanted badly enough, we got, regardless of the obstacles. When we really wanted to use, we got the job done, didn't we? Live in the now, and create the new you and your new future.

To stay in the present, look towards your future and learn from your history. I promise you, this will help you be successful.

Don't Forget:

No Recovery, No Life Worth Living.

Meetings

Self-help groups, such as AA/NA/GA/OA* suggest 90 meetings in 90 days. It is important to get a sponsor, preferably someone with at least three years of recovery, who has worked the steps and is still active in the program. This way, they can help you avoid the pitfalls of recovery. Going to AA/NA/GA/OA is an ordeal for some; they don't like the people, the place, the smoke, etc., but this is normal because we **AA - Alcoholics Anonymous; NA - Narcotics Anonymous; GA - Gamblers Anonymous; OA - Overeaters Anonymous** don't like change. Learn to acquire a taste for the meetings. Take the meat and leave the bones.

Examine where you ended up when you

drank or used drugs. Did you ever look at the people you were hanging out with? It is very important to be around other people with similar problems who are also fighting to rebuild their lives. Find the winners and get close to them; learn what helped them so you can help yourself. Find a meeting place where you feel most comfortable. If you don't find one, keep searching until you do. Don't give up. Remember, you went to any lengths to get your drug of choice, now do the same to get your recovery.

Goal Setting

Goal setting is very important because it creates a zest for life and builds your confidence. Start small; set short-term goals and then long-term goals. Keep in mind your main focus is on your recovery. When you complete one of your goals, be proud and give yourself a reward. You need to be careful when you are working on your goals.

Beware of being too compulsive or obsessive. This will burn you out, and you will not want to finish the job.

Please slow down and take it easy. It took a long time to get sick, and it will take time to get well. When you wanted to use, you had a plan, gathered all of your resources, and then went to any length to get the job done. So don't tell yourself, "I can't!" "I don't know how!" "I don't know what I want to do!"These are all excuses you never used when you wanted to get high. So get busy, create a life you can be proud of, and go for it!

Body Language

Become aware of how you sit and stand, because body language has a lot to do with how you feel. Stand and sit up straight; don't slump. Do you remember when others would tell us this and how we hated it? Funny thing, what was told to us is quite valid. When your vertebrae are straight, your energy flows smoothly and uninterrupted. When you walk with your head up, you carry a sense of confidence, you are sure of yourself, and your energy is flowing smoothly. This will assist you in having a better sense of well-being.

When you sit or walk with your head down or your posture is all twisted, it is telling people that something is wrong and you are not okay. This can and does block smooth energy flow. So be aware of your posture.

Breathing

Most people never think about how they breathe or just take it for granted. Learn to breathe deeply from below your navel, breathing slowly in and out. By breathing slowly and deeply, you help calm yourself in times of stress. Posture and breathing are very important, so please don't take them for granted. Awareness helps our lives become more manageable.

Self-Talk

Be careful of how you talk to yourself. Never put yourself down or call yourself stupid, lazy, etc. This is called negative self-talk. When you do this, repeat to yourself, "Cancel, cancel, cancel." Do your best not to say negative statements about yourself or anyone else because this brings negative energy back to you.

If you find yourself obsessing on using drugs, alcohol, or any behavior that is not going to benefit you in recovery, change where you are, call someone, and immediately do something to create movement. Don't allow your negative self-talk to keep talking.

When you focus on negative thoughts, stop and do your best to fill the negative with positive, because if you don't, your negative thoughts will soon come alive. Stop playing helpless. Take charge of your feelings, or they will take charge of you. Positive self-talk helps more than you will ever know.

Positive Affirmations

Positive affirmations are a very good way to reinforce your positive thinking. I suggest you buy those little post-it notes and write down some positive affirmations. Place these little "stickies" on your bathroom mirror, by your dresser, or in prominent places. Here are a few affirmations you may want to consider: "Be kind," "This too shall pass," "Get out of yourself," "Stay focused," and my favorite, "Gratitude instead of attitude." Don't judge it, just do it and see if it works for you!

Expectations

When you expect something and don't get it, you may be disappointed. Often this starts the process of beating ourselves up and dragging all of our failures to the present. Then we play the victim and the *poor me's* start. You will eventually medicate yourself with food, sex, work, exercise, money, etc.—anything not to feel or think. Instead of medicating yourself, you need to enjoy the journey and not be attached to the result.

Here is the addict's favorite song. "If only I had done that," "If only she/he would be different," "If only my family understood what I'm going through," and on and on. Enough with the song—you're right where you need to be. All you have to do is give time, time, be consistent, and build a strong foundation in recovery. Build a powerful support system, and continue to reach out to the winners, asking them how they felt early in recovery. Find out what people did or how they stopped putting expectations on other people and themselves. If you keep asking, sooner or later you'll find your truth, and it will set you free.

Projection

Leave projection to the people who work with crystal balls. We love to project, and often it doesn't come out the way we expected. Because things didn't happen fast enough, didn't happen at all, or happened and it wasn't what we expected, we get angry with everyone, ourselves included. So when you project outcomes, it usually never turns out the way you want. Then you work yourself up and are stressed out over something that has not even happened.

The future is up to your Higher Power, not you. Do as much as you can and let go of your obsession, because if you hold on to it, you will eventually get sick or high. Being obsessed with the outcome and thinking you are sure you know what is going to happen can create unwarranted fears. Stay grounded by meditating, talking to your Higher Power, and enjoying the journey. You never know when your journey will end. If you learn to stay at peace within yourself the best you can and as often as you can, you then learn to live life one day at a time with a positive attitude.

Resentments

Resentments can only hurt us, not help. Reliving anger and pain and displacing it on other people will only cause us to become depressed. Next, we will use a substance to ease the pain. We can't change people, places, or things, but we can change ourselves. Self-righteousness never worked for anyone who was successful in recovery.

I know that this relationship is the key to my happiness. Now if I can just find that door, we'll be home free.

We love to be forgiven for our misdeeds, but we just about refuse to forgive others.

If you do not share how you are feeling and how you allowed someone to get under your skin, resentments will be created. All you have to do is talk to your Higher Power and ask for help and guidance. Say the serenity prayer: "God, grant me the serenity to accept the things I can not change, the courage to change the things I can, and the wisdom to know the difference." You can't change that person, but you can change yourself, and knowing this is the difference. I know you're probably saying "Yeah, sure!" Let's look at some options.

We can ruin a good time, a relationship, a job, a career, and who knows what else, but you don't have to sabotage your serenity over something you cannot change. Learn to forgive if you want to attract forgiveness. That is what it is all about.

Anger

Addicts and alcoholics are often addicted to excitement and adrenaline rushes. Anger is a primary example of one feeling an addict knows and knows well. When you get angry, a rush of adrenaline flows through your body, and it is equal to the rush you got when you were getting high. Like chasing the drug, we start to chase the adrenaline rush, and we start to create chaos with everyone and everything. This is a superficial feeling that hides the truth. The pain, fear, frustration, guilt, and shame are the feelings that anger really covers up.

Anger keeps you sick and away from your true feelings. You can also get a distorted pleasure from anger, as though it was a justification to be right and make people, places, and things wrong. When you do this, you take the focus off yourself and tell yourself that it's everyone else's fault. If you want to get angry at something, get angry at your disease.

Take the energy and use it to your benefit. When you feel yourself bubbling up, remove yourself from the situation and call someone like your sponsor, therapist, or go to a meeting. Then write down the feelings, how it affected you, what you did about it, what you felt like afterwards, and what you need to change.

Anger has always worked against me because I would get out of control. I allowed my anger to control me. Being right was more important then getting my needs met! Boy, do I know how to shortchange myself. Create strategies on how to cope with your anger before it takes control of you.

Anger management is part of a good recovery.

Blaming

Recovery is a beautiful journey that has its ups and downs. Follow a program of recovery, and you'll enjoy your ups and successfully work through your downs. Blaming others for your misfortunes does nothing for you or your recovery. The only thing you can do is to focus on yourself and change what you need to. Don't waste time trying to change others and prove them wrong; just work on yourself and focus on your recovery.

I promise you, the longer you stay clean, everything will become clear, and you will feel a lot better about yourself and others. Take responsibility for your actions. Do your best to be kind instead of right. When we take responsibility for our choices, we learn from our mistakes and grow. With a little practice, you'll be amazed. Now get busy and change the things you can.

**I refuse to be a puppet on a string. Today I
will take responsibility for my own life.**

Relationships

Relationships are one of the most difficult situations you will face in recovery. If you're not in one, do your best to stay out of one until you get better acquainted with the new you. Deal with some of your issues: control, anger, jealousy, possessiveness, etc. Now we don't expect you to never feel this way, but through working a program (12 steps) and seeing a therapist, you will eventually learn to deal with these feelings and not react to them.

Early in recovery, some addicts try to either repair or get into a new relationship. Getting into a new relationship is a disaster early in recovery, because you must work on the relationship with yourself before having a relationship with anyone else. If you are already in a relationship, utilize a therapist to assist you in rebuilding your relationship with your significant other. Be prepared; this may take a long time and/or it may not even happen. Please do not put your relationship ahead of your recovery. This is where you have to be a little selfish. Without recovery, there is nothing. If it were meant to be, it would be. Get all the help you can from your sponsor, support group, therapist, psychiatrist, etc.

Many relapses are directly related to people getting into or trying to fix relationships with their significant others. Get your priorities straight. When you learn to love yourself, loving others falls right into place.

There are different types of relationships. Those of you who feel resentments towards your fathers, mothers, sisters, or brothers need to focus on yourselves first. Stop wasting your time trying to change them. Wake up; the only person you can change is you, and you know how difficult that is. There is positive and negative in everyone.

Adopt the positive traits, and learn from the negative ones. There are no mistakes. Whether you believe it or not, life dealt you the lessons you needed to learn. If you want to play "poor me" or "a victim," go for it! I can tell you that I wasted a lot of years feeling sorry for myself; all I managed to do was go deeper into my addiction and become angrier at my life and others. Learn to live along spiritual lines, and pray for understanding and the gift of being able to forgive.

Sexual Desires

Hey! Guess what? It's normal to have sexual desires. The only problem is that most addicts equate sex with drugs. In other words, sex either becomes a drug, or when we have sex, we need drugs. So what is an addict to do? First of all, we need to get our priorities straight. Recovery must come first, in short, do not let lust or anything else get in the way of your recovery.

Being addicted to anything takes us away from our path of recovery. Don't have sex with anyone who drinks or uses drugs or is a danger to your new lifestyle of being drug and alcohol free. If the person is a social drinker, ask them not to drink when they're around you. Please don't act like you can handle it. First of all, there's no need to test yourself, and second, why risk it, even if drinking is not your drug of choice? Learn from those who came before you. Being stubborn never really worked for any of us.

Amends

In early recovery, you may want to make amends for the harm you have caused and the people you have hurt, but do not jump the gun. You will start to feel good about yourself and think you can make amends, but take it slow. The steps are in order for a reason.

We are still fragile when we are early in recovery. We may have hurt a lot of people and want to say we are sorry. We think just because we are sober, people are going to forgive us or accept our apologies—wake up! This is not always going to be the case. When people don't accept our apologies, we get hurt, and we may feel shame or remorse. This can sit in the pit of our stomachs, cause us to eventually get high, and destroy our lives once again.

Amends are measured by what we do and how our behaviors have changed, rather than by what we say. "I'm sorry," gets old after awhile. Do the program the way it is laid out and the rest will follow. Where there is fear, there is no faith. Without faith, there is no hope.

Good Job, Keep Reading

Trust

Some people poke and prod us and continuously ask if we used drugs or alcohol. Do not expect trust right away. Allow people to heal. Some people slip up. When someone goes back to using or old behaviors, they may lose the trust of their peers and any confidence they may have established. The person may lose the belief that they can succeed in recovery. Sometimes you are not quite sure if you can continue without a mood-altering substance, so be patient. Don't play the victim and say to yourself, "No matter what I do, it's never good enough," or "I can't do this." Get out of your self-centeredness, and tell yourself you are good enough and you can do it!

You need to realize this is a process, not an event. Change your response, and you change your outcome. As they say in the program, "Give time, time!" Don't you just love this saying? Give yourself a break, believe it until it becomes believable, and believe me, it will! Trust in yourself. Eventually, people will too. How long will this take? I don't know. That's up to you and your Higher Power.

Asking for Help

Last but not least, there are those of us who believe we know what we have to do. Unfortunately, asking for help is not part of the plan. There is something you may want to consider. What is the payoff for not asking for help? Using, of course. These types of people help everyone except themselves. They do this because they do not want to take a look at themselves. In most cases, they do not realize that is why they do this. They are the martyrs of addiction, the victims of life. It is okay to help yourself, it is okay to be kind to yourself, and it is okay to love yourself, because you can't give away what you don't have.

By asking for help and taking a risk, you learn how to deal with rejection, and you learn to let people help you. You also learn how to be courageous and face your fears. Best of all, you help other people to get out of themselves by helping you. It is all a matter of perception, my friend. Isn't that what life is all about?

Calling for Help

When feeling low and no place to turn, call us at (305) 945–8384 or 1–800–559–9503. This is a 24-hour a day hot line. We can't keep what we have unless we give it away. If you don't reach out and ask for help because you feel stupid for calling, how can we help you? So don't act stupid: call if you need to, or at least reach out to someone who understands addiction.

Triggers

Stay away from people, places, and things that trigger your wanting to use or have past memories of using. Hanging around bars or drinking and drugging friends can and will cause you to relapse. Be careful. Our disease is cunning, baffling, and powerful; it will try and take us out any way it can. This disease is that fleeting thought or any number of thoughts that take us back to our old ways. It tells us that it was not that bad. Be careful when you get one of these thoughts; please tell somebody right away. Start telling on your disease! It really makes a difference. We have what is called selective memory. Addicts forget the agony and the shame of using. Don't allow yourself to be fooled one more time. See it for what it really is: death, institutions, jails, as well as loneliness, shame, and guilt. It doesn't have to end this way. It's up to you.

Coping with Urges

When you get an urge that doesn't want to go away, consider not pushing it away. Go to another room or safe place and think the urge through. Start with what you would have to do in order to get that drug or drink. Think it all the way to when it finally runs out. Remind yourself of what it felt like to run out of the drug and want more. Remember what you had to do to get more and how that made you feel. All that shame and guilt that sat in the pit of your stomach. Remember how you were downright disgusted with yourself, how you hurt yourself, and especially how you hurt the people that really loved you. Whatever it was that initiated your response to destroy yourself one more time was definitely not worth it. So if this ever happens, think it through and immediately call someone safe: a close friend, your sponsor, and/or your therapist.

Never allow yourself to get hungry, angry, lonely, or tired for any length of time. Get proper rest, 6–8 hours a night. Do your best to eat at regular times each day. Don't isolate yourself. When you do, your mind will tend to become a dangerous place to hang out. Before you know it, the using thought has passed. Remember the saying, "This too shall pass."

Strategy for the Day

◊   Get up in the morning and say a prayer to your Higher Power. If not, pray for

◊   G.O.D. (Good Orderly Direction).

◊   Take five minutes to meditate in order to prepare for your day.

◊   Do your best to maintain positive self-talk. That means no negative thoughts, words, or actions. Okay, I know it's difficult! Just do your best. Seek progress, not perfection.

◊   Exercise: walking, swimming, weight lifting, etc.

◊   Stay away from caffeine and drink decaffeinated coffee.

◊   Go to meetings and sit in the front. Get to the meeting (AA/NA/GA/OA) 5 minutes early. At the meeting, if you are unsure of what you want to say, then just raise your hand and tell everyone that you're new and are just learning how to share.

Suggestions

Get telephone numbers from other members and practice calling them. Get a sponsor who is at least 3 years clean and is active in the program. Meet with him/her at least once a week (male sponsor with male, female sponsor with female). After going to 90 meetings in 90 days, you can continue to go everyday or cut back on your meetings. My suggestion is to go to 4–5 meetings per week. Work your steps. It is a therapeutic tool that will assist you on your journey.

Stay connected to the winners. Get involved. First build a strong foundation, and if you have to change anything after a year, then do it. It takes approximately 18 months before your thoughts become clearly focused. Don't forget when you stop using drugs, you then begin to heal. What you're dealing with is called post acute withdrawal syndrome. So give time, time. When you end your day, meditate and reflect on your day. Notice the difference between how you feel about yourself when you do uphold your program and values compared to how you feel when you compromise yourself.

Carry yourself with your shoulders back and head up high. It's difficult to feel depressed when your posture is held this way. I don't expect you to believe me, but just do it. If it doesn't work for you, don't do it.

Read these suggestions over and over again, and do your best to follow them; don't worry if you don't do them perfectly, just do the work the best you can. The benefits will be 100-fold, I promise you! Do the best you can in following these suggestions; they're not meant to hurt you or control you, just to help you to help yourself.

My hope for you is for you to become all that you can and to be the person God intended you to be. May your Higher Power continue to guide you on your journey, and remember, there are no coincidences. May these words of addicts and alcoholics who have come before you give you the strength and the courage to follow through and enjoy life one day at a time.

Relapse History

Please fill out your relapse history on the following two pages so you may see the sequence of events that lead towards making poor choices. When you are aware of your pathology, only then can you intervene and make changes that are necessary to stay on your path of recovery. So be thorough—your life depends upon it!

Look for your patterns; we all have them. Find the ones that are destructive, and also look for the ones that are beneficial. You might want to ask someone to help you to be objective. Please don't wait. Get busy!

Relapse History

Name: _____

Age:_____

Drugs of choice: _____

How long have you been clean from drugs and alcohol?

_____

_____

How much treatment have you had?_____

Number of different centers you attended. _____

_____

Length of time in each? _____

How many times did you relapse?_____

What happened before you relapsed?_____

_____

_____What happened during your outing?_____

_____What were your consequences after you relapsed?

_____

_____

_____

What caused you to get back on track?_____

_____

_____

How did you feel when you made it back on the recovery path? _____

_____

_____

_____

_____

Part II

12 Ways to Be Good to Yourself

1. Be part of the solution, instead of the problem. Refuse to beat yourself up anymore. What good does it do anyway . . . besides, it hurts.

2. Take it slow and easy, the new path you have chosen takes time to get used to. Learn to be patient or at least tolerant. Things change when you are consistent. The change is not about immediate gratification; it's about long term meaningful gratification, not short term fixes that don't really work.

3. Remember to give yourself positive strokes along the way. God knows how difficult it is to stay on a path of recovery, so be good to yourself; you've earned your accolades the same way you've earned your pain and suffering.

4. When you have loving thoughts towards yourself and others, you'll attract good energies back to yourself. I know you know what happens when our thoughts and actions are impure; we need only look around us at the messes our addictions brought upon us to be assured of this truth. Therefore, cultivate those good thoughts. Let them grow and help to heal you. Remember—progress, not perfection.

5. Refuse to criticize yourself or anyone else. Self-righteousness never was very becoming, and

besides, all it gets you is rejection and low self-esteem. Addicts seem to enjoy being on a fault-finding mission with themselves and others.

6. Treat yourself to a hot bath, and light a scented candle; put on your favorite relaxing music, and take a healthy break from the world. Oh! Don't worry, all your problems will still be there, and you can pick them back up if you choose to.

7. Go for a walk in the park or on the beach—anyplace where you can get back in touch with your gratitude for just being alive, clean, and sober. Reconnecting with the beauty of nature is a blessing in itself.

8. Seek out some warm and friendly conversations. If you can afford it, arrange a relaxing massage, along with some pleasant fragrances. Practice feeling good. God knows, we practice hard enough feeling bad.

9. Complete just one thing you said you were going to do. It doesn't matter how trivial. Just feel how it feels to keep your word again, to yourself or to others.

10. Maintain an attitude of gratitude, for humbleness is definitely the way to spirituality and is a prerequisite for being open-minded and willing to change.

11. Learn to compliment yourself and others. It's a beautiful way of saying, "I notice your efforts."

So often we notice our faults, and everyone else's; it's time for changes. Appreciate life, and life will show its gratitude.

12. The ultimate way to feel good, I believe, is to reach out and help another human being. A phone call goes a long way. Just lending an ear to someone who is reaching out. It is the simple things that seem to have the most impact.

A New Life Worth Living

Confused on how to go about living a life of recovery? You are definitely not alone. Many before you had the same concerns. Will I be able to live without drugs and be happy? Can I maintain a recovery lifestyle? Where does my life go from here? So many questions, so few answers. Can I do it? Do I want to do it? (Recovery). The questions will keep appearing. The good news is that most of your questions will be answered as time goes by.

Learning how to live takes time; being in a hurry will not make it happen any faster. Did you ever stop and think that you are already doing exactly what you need to do? Once you create movement, you then create change. The moment change occurs, opportunity occurs along with all kinds of possibilities. Staying free from drugs/alcohol and risky behaviors creates an environment for healthy progress. Remember—progress, not perfection.

The program of recovery has an abundance of incredibly helpful information, which is based on favorable results: The knowledge of how to live and enjoy life on life's terms. Reach out to those who have come before you. Seek out the winners, the ones with long time abstinence, as well as a lifestyle of recovery. Recovery is not just about drugs and alcohol; it's about spirituality, balance, and finding your purpose in life, in order to become all that your creator intended you to be.

When you seek out the winners of recovery, remember that they are human beings who are struggling with their own character defects. Please don't place them on a pedestal, for you will only become disappointed. Your job is to keep what works for you and discard the rest. Remember that you have choices. Take a risk and ask for help. It may be uncomfortable, but it won't kill you. The consequences of not asking for the help you need can and will be quite severe: death, institutions, and jails. And worst of all, living with your shame and guilt until you die. Following these simple suggestions will give you a life beyond your wildest dreams. You see, I know this to be true, I have that life!

Steps to Building a New Life

1. Maintain a recovery lifestyle. Follow the suggestions in this book, as well as the self help text (AA/NA/GA/OA).

2. Turn your focus inward. Become grounded in who you would like to become. Write down your values, your likes, and dislikes. Write down your wants and needs. A want is something you would like. A need is a necessity. If you don't know what you want or need, then write down all the things you don't want or need, and see what's left. Then go from there.

3. Regarding relationships, you should write down, as best you can, your character defects. Be thorough; ask people who really know you, preferably people who have your best interest at heart. Be prepared! You may not like what you hear. It's not about likes or dislikes; it's about gathering information. The more information, the better and more effective we will become with family, friends, and significant others. Keep in mind you are gathering information so you can better yourself. Reach out to your friends, relatives, and your significant other, provided you still have one. The

more information you gather, the better you can understand the changes that may need to be made. Find your weaknesses and your strengths and then reach out for help. Keep reaching out until you receive the answers you need in order for you to grow and change.

4. It has been my experience that addicts and alcoholics are usually very intelligent. It doesn't matter whether we learned it in the streets or in school; we learned how to live and survive in the world in spite of the odds. Now it is time to improve ourselves and enjoy a much better quality of life, free from whatever behavior or substance that we allowed to keep us prisoner. By exploring who we are and what we became, along with what we like and dislike, only then can we live the quality of life that God intended us to have.

5. Patience, consistency, commitment, and desire are just a few of the qualities we need to develop in order to be successful in anything. Keep reaching out and looking inward; more will be revealed.

6. Thoughts and ideas are great; reaching out to others is wonderful. Reading and educating yourself is noble, but without follow-up, all that good intent and initiative is for naught. Taking action is what brings cohesion to our lives. Because if you don't put all of this knowledge to use, what value does it hold? How can it possibly help you on your journey? I believe you need to ask yourself "What

is preventing me from putting into action what I have learned?" Remember, it is a "we" program, not an "I" program. You never have to do anything alone again.

Negative Self-Talk that Prevents Us from Benefiting from Self-Help Groups

One of the real barriers to recovery is our own mind! Negative self talk prevents us from benefiting from self help groups. Be alert to some of the following negative inner dialogues that often "tell us" to fail:

1. "These people are much sicker than I could ever be. I definitely don't belong here."

2. "This is a cult of fanatics. These people need to get a life!"

3. "Most of the people are probably drinking or getting high. I can't believe they are not doing anything."

4. "I can't see how listening to the stories can help me to stop using. It will probably just cause me to want to use more."

5. "I've never hit a 'bottom' like some of the people describe; I can't relate. I've been successful, have money, and have never robbed anyone . . . *What am I doing here?*"

6. "I'm not stupid. I know what I have to do. I know I can quit using. I don't need someone else's help or support. I'm no weakling."

7. "I just did a little too much. I'll simply limit myself to smoking pot and drinking only beer. I never got into too much trouble with only pot or beer."

8. "These people are religious freaks. I don't want to be part of this new religion. Where is God when you need him, anyway?"

9. "I don't do street drugs (yuck); *My* drugs are legal and acceptable to society. Besides, my (expensive) doctor prescribed them for me. So I went a little overboard a few times . . . Big Deal!"

10. "These people's problems are nothing like mine. I only have two DUI's, not four like the guy next to me. My wife and I are only separated because she makes a big deal of my staying out getting high. At least I don't beat my wife like the guy in front of me. I would never get high with these kinds of people. The crack houses I go to have classier people than this."

Appendices

Holistic Addiction Treatment Vitamins

(Vitamins can be found at www.helpaddicts.com)

1. Anti-Anxiety Formula / Sleep: This formula is designed to assist in creating a normal sleep pattern and calm the nervous system.

2. Vitamin B-6 (pyridoxine HCI): involved in the formation of body proteins and structural compounds, including chemical transmitters in the brain. Vitamin B6 is also critical in maintaining hormonal balance and proper immune function. Deficiency of Vitamin B6 is characterized by depression, glucose intolerance, anemia, impaired nerve function, cracking of the lips and tongue, and seborrhea or eczema. [1]

3. Valerian Root—Valerian (*Nervous*): has been used as a sleep aid for over 1,000 years. Its ability to help relax the central nervous system, promote feelings of calm, decrease levels of anxiety and stress, and enhance sleep are known to millions the world over. Unlike some prescription

sleep aids, valerian is not known to cause morning grogginess and is non-addictive. Time-release technology offers a steady release of valerian for 6–8 hours, ensuring better, more restful sleep.

4. Skullcap herb: one of the most widely relevant nervines available. It relaxes states of nervous tension while at the same time renewing and revitalizing the central nervous system. It has a specific use in the treatment of seizure and hysterical states as well as epilepsy.[2]

5. L-Theanine: a non-protein amino acid mainly found naturally in the green tea plant (Camellia sinensis). L-theanine is the predominant amino acid in green tea and makes up 50% of the total free amino acids in the plant. The amino acid constitutes between 1% and 2% of the dry weight of green tea leaves. L-theanine is considered the main component responsible for the taste of green tea, which in Japanese is called umami. L-theanine is marketed in Japan as a nutritional supplement for mood modulation.[3]

6. Passion Flower: Bears small berry-like fruit called granadilla or water lemon. The plant is native to North, Central, and South America. While primarily tropical, some of its 400 species can grow in colder climates. The plant is also nicknamed Maypop, descriptive of the popping sound the fruit makes when mashed. Passion Flower was first investigated scientifically less than 100

years ago when it was found to possess an analgesic (pain-killing) property, and to prevent, without side effects, sleeplessness caused by brain inflammation. Since then, the sedative properties of Passion Flower have been observed and documented in many studies. Primary chemical constituents of this herb include alkaloids (harman, harmine, harmaline, harmol, harmalol), flavonoids (apigenin, luteolin, quercitin, rutin), flavone glycosides, sterols, sugars, and gums. The flavonoids in Passion Flower are primarily responsible for its relaxing and anti-anxiety effects.

7. Chamomile: One of the safest medicinal herbs, chamomile is a soothing, gentle relaxant that has been shown to work for a variety of complaints from stress to menstrual cramps. This herb has a satisfying, apple-like aroma and flavor (the name chamomile is derived from the Greek kamai melon, meaning ground apple), and it's most often taken as a delicious, mild therapeutic tca.

8. Melatonin: a hormone (N-acetyl-5 methoxytryptamine) produced especially at night in the pineal gland, a structure in the brain. Its secretion is stimulated by the dark and inhibited by light. Tryptophan is converted to serotonin and finally converted to melatonin, which is an Indole.

9. Lemon Balm: has mild sedative properties and has been used to relieve gas, reduce fever, and increase perspiration. The volatile oil contains cit-

ral, citronellal, eugenol acetate and geraniol. Both oil and hot water extracts of the leaves have been shown to possess strong antibacterial and antiviral qualities.[1]

25.00 mg	Vitamin B-6 (pyridoxine HCI)
800.00 mg	Valerian Root
250.00 mg	Skullcap herb
50.00 mg	L-Theanine
40.00 mg	Passion Flower
25.00 mg	Chamomile
1.00 mg	Melatonin
100.00 mg	Lemon Balm

For More Information See The Following Web Sites

◊ http://www.iherb.com /

◊ http://herbalformulas.com/

◊ http://www.gettingwell.com/

◊ http://www.viable-herbal.com

◊ http://www.ces.ncsu.edu/

MULTI-VITAMIN MINERAL "SELF-DEFENSE"

This formula is designed to help balance the nervous system and strengthen the whole body.

1. Copper (sulfate): The human body contains only 70 to 80 mg of copper in total, but it's an essential part of many important enzymes. Copper's possible role in treating disease is based on the fact that these enzymes can't do their jobs without it.[1]

2. Manganese (sulfate): Our bodies contain only a very small amount of manganese, but this metal is important as a constituent of many key enzymes. The chemical structure of these enzymes is interesting: large protein molecules cluster around a tiny atom of metal.

3. Manganese plays a particularly important role as part of the natural antioxidant enzyme super oxide dismutase (SOD), which helps fight damaging free radicals. It also helps energy metabolism, thyroid function, blood sugar control, and normal skeletal growth.

4. Chromium (picolinate): Chromium is a mineral the body needs in very small amounts, but it plays a significant role in human nutrition. Chromium's most important function in the body is to help regulate the amount of glucose (sugar) in the blood. Insulin plays a starring role in this fundamental biological process by regulating the movement of glucose out of the blood and into cells. Scientists believe that insulin uses chromium as an assistant (technically, a cofactor) to "unlock the door" to the cell membrane, thus allowing glucose to enter the cell.

5. Molybdenum (Na molybdenate): Small amounts of this element are essential.

6. Potassium (chloride): Potassium is one of the major electrolytes in your body, along with sodium and chloride. Potassium and sodium work together like a molecular seesaw: when the level of one goes up, the other goes down. All together, these three dissolved minerals play an intimate chemical role in every function of your body.

7. Vanadium (chelate): Vanadium, a mineral, is named after the Scandinavian goddess of beauty,

youth, and luster. Taking vanadium will not make you beautiful, youthful, and lustrous, but evidence from animal studies suggests it may be an essential micronutrient. That is, your body may need it, but in very low doses.

8. Boron (chelate): Boron aids in the proper metabolism of vitamins and minerals involved with bone development, such as calcium, copper, magnesium, and vitamin D. In addition, boron appears to affect estrogen and possibly testosterone as well, hormones that affect bone health. On this basis, boron has been suggested for preventing or treating osteoporosis. However, there have been no clinical studies to evaluate the potential benefits of boron supplements for any bone-related conditions.

On the basis of similarly weak evidence, boron is often added to supplements intended for the treatment of osteoarthritis. Boron has also been proposed as a sports supplement, based on its effects on hormones. However, studies have, as yet, failed to find evidence that it helps increase muscle mass or enhances performance.

9. Choline (bitartrate): Choline has only recently been recognized as an essential nutrient. Choline is part of the neurotransmitter acetylcholine, which plays a major role in the brain; for this reason, many studies have been designed to look at choline's role in brain function.

Choline functions as a part of a major biochemical process in the body called methylation; choline acts as a methyl donor.

Until recently, it was thought that the body could use other substances to substitute for choline, such as folate, vitamins B_6 and B_{12}, and the amino acid methionine. But recent evidence has finally shown that, for some people, adequate choline supplies cannot be maintained by other nutrients and must be obtained independently through diet or supplements.

800.00 IU Vitamin A (betatene*)
80.00 mg Vitamin C (Ester C)
80.00 IU Vitamin E (Tocopherols)
5.00 mg Thiamin (Vitamin B1)

** Spirulina, Choline Bitartrate, Bee Pollen, Citrus Bioflavonoids, Ginkgo Biloba Leaf Ext 24%, Panax Ginseng Root, PABA, Gotu Kola Herb, CoQ10, Betaine HCI, Inositol, Papain 1:2,000, Bromelain 600 GDU, Hesperidin, Lipase 1500 LU, Rutin, Licorice Root and Octacosanol.

9. Vitamin A: Vitamin A plays an important role in vision, bone growth, reproduction, cell division and cell differentiation. It helps maintain the surface linings of the eyes and the respiratory, urinary, and intestinal tracts. When those linings break down, bacteria can enter the body and cause infection. Vitamin A also helps maintain the integrity of skin and mucous membranes that function as a barrier to bacteria and viruses. Vitamin A helps regulate the immune system.

The immune system helps prevent or fight off infections by making white blood cells that destroy harmful bacteria and viruses. Vitamin A may help lymphocytes, a type of white blood cell that fights infections, function more effectively.

10. Vitamin C (Ester C): Ester-C™ is a patented form of Vitamin C that is pH-balanced and time-released. It is a patented form of ascorbyl palmi-

tate. An ester, in general, is the combination of an acid and an alcohol. With Ester-C™, the acid is ascorbic acid (vitamin C). Ester-C™ is the premium brand of vitamin C esters available. It differs from other Vitamin C's in that it will not give you an acid stomach and it will give you the benefits of Vitamin C over a longer period of time. It is also more bioavailable than other Vitamin C's. [2]

Vitamin C is required for the synthesis of collagen, an important structural component of blood vessels, tendons, ligaments, and bone. Vitamin C also plays an important role in the synthesis of the neurotransmitter, norepinephrine. Neurotransmitters are critical to brain function and are known to affect mood. In addition, vitamin C is required for the synthesis of carnitine, a small molecule that is essential for the transport of fat to cellular organelles called mitochondria, for conversion to energy Recent research also suggests that vitamin C is involved in the metabolism of cholesterol to bile acids, which may have implications for blood cholesterol levels and the incidence of gallstones .[3]

11. Vitamin E (Tocopherols): Vitamin E is any of several fat soluble vitamins that are chemically tocopherols. Vitamin E is a popular and powerful antioxidant. Vitamin E is effective in preventing the oxidation of polyunsaturated fatty acids. Additionally, Vitamin E is helpful in the prevention of oxidation in the lungs, where strong oxi-

dizing agents nitrogen dioxide and ozone, components of air pollution, are particularly harmful to people exercising. Vitamin E protects white and red blood cells, helping the body's immune system.

12. Thiamin (Vitamin B1): The need for Thiamin (Vitamin B1) in the body is mainly for the breakdown and utilization of carbohydrates and fats. As discussed earlier, carbohydrates (as glucose) are the body's main source of energy. Every cell in our body is dependent on glucose produced for energy. However, the body's ability to convert carbohydrates into glucose is interdependent with enzymes and coenzymes. For example, acting as coenzyme, Thiamin works in converting carbohydrates into glucose for energy, and every single cell of your body requires that energy. [4]

13. Riboflavin (Vitamin B2): It is required by the body to use oxygen and the metabolism of amino acids, fatty acids, and carbohydrates. Riboflavin is further needed to activate vitamin B6 (pyridoxine), helps to create niacin, and assists the adrenal gland. It may be used for red blood cell formation, antibody production, cell respiration, and growth.

14. Niacinamide: Vitamin B3 is required for cell respiration, helps in the release of energy and metabolism of carbohydrates, fats, and proteins, proper circulation and healthy skin, functioning of the nervous system, and normal secretion of bile

and stomach fluids. It is used in the synthesis of sex hormones, treating schizophrenia and other mental illnesses, and is a memory-enhancer.

15. Pyridoxine HCl (Vitamin B6): Vitamin B6 is involved in the formation of body proteins and structural compounds, including chemical transmitters in the brain. Vitamin B6 is also critical in maintaining hormonal balance and proper immune function. Deficiency of Vitamin B6 is characterized by depression, glucose intolerance, anemia, impaired nerve function, cracking of the lips and tongue, and seborrhea or eczema.

16. Folate (folic acid): Folic acid works along with vitamin B12 and vitamin C to help the body digest and utilize proteins and to synthesize new proteins when they are needed. It is necessary for the production of red blood cells and for the synthesis of DNA (which controls heredity and is used to guide the cell in its daily activities).

Folic acid also helps with tissue growth and cell function. In addition, it helps to increase appetite when needed and stimulates the formation of digestive acids.

17. Vitamin B12: It helps maintain healthy nerve cells and red blood cells, and is also needed to make DNA, the genetic material in all cells (1–4). Vitamin B12 is bound to the protein in food. Hydrochloric acid in the stomach releases B12 from protein during digestion. Once released, B12

combines with a substance called intrinsic factor (IF) before it is absorbed into the bloodstream.

18. Biotin: Biotin is a water-soluble member of the B-complex group of vitamins and is commonly referred to as vitamin H. The biochemical acts as a carrier for carbon dioxide in the pyruvate carboxylase reaction, where biotin is linked to the epsilon-amino group of a lysine residue in the enzyme.

Biotin is necessary for both metabolism and growth in humans, particularly with reference to production of fatty acids, antibodies, digestive enzymes, and in niacin (vitamin B-3) metabolism. Food sources for biotin are liver, kidney, soy flour, egg yolk, cereal, and yeast. There are suggestions that biotin is also capable of curing baldness, alleviating muscle pain and depression, and functions as a cure for dermatitis, although there is no substantial evidence for any of these claims. Biotin deficiency results in fatigue, depression, nausea, muscle pains, hair loss, and anemia.[6]

19. Pantothenic acid: Pantothenic acid (PA), a B-complex vitamin, is essential for humans and animals for growth, reproduction, and normal physiological functions. It is a precursor of the coenzymes, CoA and acyl carrier protein of fatty acid synthase, which are involved in more than 100 different metabolic pathways including energy metabolism of carbohydrates, proteins and lipids,

and the synthesis of lipids, neurotransmitters, steroid hormones, porphyrins, and hemoglobin.

20. Calcium (carbonate & citrate): Calcium is essential to many body functions, including the transmission of nerve impulses, the regulation of muscle contraction and relaxation (including of the heart), blood clotting, and various metabolic activities. Calcium is also necessary for maintaining strong bones and is commonly prescribed to prevent and treat postmenopausal osteoporosis (bone thinning). Vitamin D, which aids in the absorption of calcium from the intestine, is often prescribed along with calcium supplements to prevent or treat osteoporosis. (Indeed, some calcium supplement tablets contain vitamin D.)

21. Iodine (potassium iodide): Iodine may be used when it is desirable to maintain a high level of beneficial iodides in the thyroid gland. Iodide is a form of iodine that is permanently taken up by the thyroid gland. This product also supports the body's normal detoxification processes, including the removal of heavy metals.[8]

22. Magnesium (oxide): Magnesium is an essential nutrient, meaning that your body needs it for healthy functioning. It is found in significant quantities throughout the body and used for numerous purposes, including muscle relaxation, blood clotting, and the manufacture of ATP (adenosine triphosphate, the body's main energy molecule).

23. Zinc (aspartate): Zinc is an important element that is found in every cell in the body. More than 300 enzymes in the body need zinc in order to function properly. Although the amount of zinc we need in our daily diet is tiny, it's very important that we get it. However, the evidence suggests that many of us do not get enough.

24. Selenium (sodium selenite): Selenium is a trace mineral that our bodies use to produce glutathione peroxidase. Glutathione peroxidase is part of the body's antioxidant defense system; it works with vitamin E to protect cell membranes from damage caused by dangerous, naturally occurring substances known as free radicals.

For More Information See The Following Web Sites

◊   http://healthinfo.healthgate.com/

◊   http://www.health-pages.com/vc/

◊   http://lpi.oregonstate.edu/infocenter/vitamins/vitaminC/

◊   http://www.trekfit.com/

◊   http://www.iherb.com/

◊   http://micro.magnet.fsu.edu/vitamins/

◊   http://www.eagle-min.com/

◊ http://healthinfo.healthgate.com
◊ http://www.iherb.com/potassium4.html
◊ http://healthinfo.healthgate.com/
◊ http://healthinfo.healthgate.com/

MENTAL CLARITY
"SELF-DEFENSE"

This formula is designed to help the body, clear the mind, enhance thinking, and restore a healthy energy level.

1. dl-Phenylaline (DLPA): a 50/50 (equimolar) mixture of D-Phenylalanine and L-Phenylalanine. L-phenylalanine is an essential amino acid that can be converted to L-Tyrosine by a complex bio-chemical process that takes place in the liver. L-Tyrosine can be converted by neurons in the brain to dopamine and norepinephrine (noradrenaline), hormones which are depleted by stress, overwork, and certain drugs. By replenishing norepinephrine

133

in the brain, mental energy levels are enhanced, some forms of depression are alleviated, and a feeling of contentment often occurs. Because of the liver conversion necessary for L-phenylalanine to have these effects, L-Tyrosine is often faster acting. In addition, the conversion step from L-Tyrosine to norepinephrine may be enhanced if the cofactors (vitamins B6 and C) are included.[1]

2. L-Tyrosine: a nonessential *amino acid* (protein building block) that the body synthesizes from *phenylalanine,* another amino acid. Tyrosine is important to the structure of almost all proteins in the body. It is also the precursor of several neurotransmitters, including L-dopa, dopamine, norepinephrine, and epinephrine. L-tyrosine, through its effect on neurotransmitters, may affect several health conditions, including *Parkinson's disease, depression,* and other mood disorders. Studies have suggested that tyrosine may help people with depression. Preliminary findings indicate a beneficial effect of tyrosine, along with other amino acids, in people affected by dementia, including *Alzheimer's disease.*[2] Due to its role as a precursor to norepinephrine and epinephrine (two of the body's main stress-related hormones) tyrosine may also ease the adverse effects of environmental, psychosocial, and physical stress.

L-tyrosine is converted by skin cells into melanin, the dark pigment that protects against the harmful effects of ultraviolet light. Thyroid hormones, which have a role in almost every process in the body, also contain tyrosine as part of their structure.

3. L-Glutamine: The extremely popular amino acid L-Glutamine can be found in protein powders, beans, meats, fish, poultry, dairy products, and of course, L-Glutamine supplements. Glutamine is highly in demand throughout the body. For years, athletes and bodybuilders have been looking for a product to help them recover faster from workouts and competition, keep their muscles well hydrated for maximum growth, and provide numerous other benefits in the muscle building process. In recent years, most athletes have come to understand the benefits of L-Glutamine.

L-Glutamine is the most abundant amino acid in the body and makes up more than 60% of the intramuscular amino acid pool. L-Glutamine plays an important role in many body functions such as proper immune system function, the transfer of nitrogen between organs, precursor to DNA, and regulation of protein synthesis and degradation. Following an intense workout, your body needs to replenish glutamine stores to aid in recovery. L-Glutamine can help increase muscle cell hydration and aid in protein synthesis. These and more functions of L-Glutamine can benefit athletes and bodybuilders by improving recovery and performance.

4. Taurine: an *amino acid*-like compound and a

component of bile acids, which are used to help absorb *fats* and fat-soluble *vitamins*. Taurine also helps regulate the heartbeat, maintain cell membrane stability, and prevent brain cell over-activity.

5. Ginseng root, Korean / panax: True ginseng is in the genus Panax, which comes from the Latin word *panacea*. The type of ginseng typically used is of the species ginseng. Ginseng is used to treat a host of conditions, and, when it is taken daily, to maintain general good health. Ginseng has been shown in human studies to have a long-term anti-stress effect and to improve physical and mental performance, memory, and reaction time.

6. L-Theanine: a non-protein amino acid mainly found naturally in the green tea plant (Camellia sinensis). L-theanine is the predominant amino acid in green tea and makes up 50% of the total free amino acids in the plant. The amino acid constitutes between 1% and 2% of the dry weight of green tea leaves. L-theanine is considered the main component responsible for the taste of green tea, which in Japanese is called umami. L-theanine is marketed in Japan as a nutritional supplement for mood modulation.

7. B6 Pyridoxine HCI: Vitamin B6 (Pyridoxine) is involved in the formation of body proteins and structural compounds, including chemical transmitters in the brain. Vitamin B6 is also criti-

cal in maintaining hormonal balance and proper immune function. Deficiency of Vitamin B6 is characterized by depression, glucose intolerance, anemia, impaired nerve function, cracking of the lips and tongue, and seborrhea or eczema.

8. Ginkgo Biloba Leaf Extract: supports the memory function; ginkgo also appears to support blood circulation to the brain, thereby optimizing the amount of oxygen supplied to brain cells. It may also help increase blood flow to the extremities.

9. 5 HTP: The nutrient 5-HTP (the common name for the compound 5-hydroxytryptophan) is a derivative of the amino acid tryptophan. A mood-enhancing chemical, 5-HTP has attracted a good deal of attention lately because of its ability to increase pain tolerance, induce sleep, and affect how hunger is perceived. Unlike many other supplements (and drugs) that have molecules too large to pass from the bloodstream into the brain, molecules of 5-HTP are small enough to do so. Once in the brain, they're converted into an important nervous system chemical, or neurotransmitter, called serotonin.

The body produces its own supply of 5HTP from tryptophan, an amino acid found in high-protein foods such as chicken, fish, beef, and dairy products. Any healthy diet should include tryptophan-rich sources such as these.

270.00 mg	dl-Phenylaline
200.00 mg	L-Tyrosine
200.00 mg	L-Glutamine
100.00 mg	Taurine
25.00 mg	Ginseng root, Korean / panax
15.00 mg	L-Theanine
6.00 mg	Pyridoxine HCI
25.00 mg	Ginkgo Biloba Leaf Ext 24%
6.00 mg	5 HTP

For More Information See The Following Web Sites

◊ http:www.health-marketplace.com/

◊ http://www.vitacost.com/science/

◊ http://www.evitamins.com/

◊ http://www.gnc.com/health_notes/

◊ http://dreampharm.com/

◊ http://www.gettingwell.com/

◊ http://www.iherb.com/

◊ http://www.taoofherbs.com/

◊ http://www.wholehealthmd.com/

HEP C LIVER
"SELF-DEFENSE"

This formula is designed to help significantly lower the viral load and create more energy.

1. Vitamin C (Ester C): Ester-C™ is a patented form of Vitamin C that is pH-balanced and time-released. It is a patented form of ascorbyl palmitate. An ester, in general, is the combination of an acid and an alcohol. With Ester-C™, the acid is ascorbic acid (vitamin C). Ester-C™ is the premium brand of vitamin C esters available. It differs from other Vitamin C's in that it will not give you an acid stomach and it will give you the benefits of Vitamin C over a longer period of time. It is also more bioavailable than other Vitamin C's.

2. Phosophatidyl Choline Complex: Phytosomes are advanced forms of herbal products that are better absorbed, utilized, and, as a result, produce better results than conventional herbal extracts. Phytosomes are produced via a patented process whereby the individual components of an herbal extract are bound to phosphatidylcholine—an emulsifying compound derived from soy. Phosphatidylcholine is also one of the chief components of the membranes in our cells.

3. Milk Thistle Seed Ext.: Milk Thistle extract

promotes healthy, vibrant liver function. The liver is one of the body's most important organs, since it helps rid the body of toxins that can impair good health. The active ingredient in milk thistle thought to give it its beneficial properties is called silymarin. The extract of milk thistle provides a guaranteed potency of 80% silymarin. It is an herb from a plant found in dry rocky soil in Europe and the U.S.

4. Calcium D-glucarate - Calcium D-glucarate is the *calcium* salt of D-glucaric acid, a natural substance found in many *fruits* and *vegetables*.

Calcium D-glucarate has been shown to inhibit beta-glucuronidase, an enzyme found in certain bacteria that reside in the gut. One of the key ways in which the body eliminates toxic chemicals as well as hormones such as *estrogen* is by attaching glucuronic acid to them in the liver and then excreting this complex in the bile. Beta-glucuronidase is a bacterial enzyme that uncouples (breaks) the bond between the excreted compound and glucuronic acid. When beta-glucuronidase breaks the bond, the hormone or toxic chemical that is released is available to be reabsorbed into the body instead of being excreted. An elevated beta-glucuronidase activity is associated with an increased risk for various *cancers,* particularly hormone-dependent cancers like *breast, prostate,* and *colon.*

5. Artichoke ext 2% Cynarin: This large, thistle-like plant is native to the regions of southern Europe, North Africa, and the Canary Islands. The leaves of the plant are used medicinally. However, the roots and the immature flower heads may also contain beneficial compounds. Artichoke leaves contain a wide number of active constituents, including cynarin, 1,3 dicaffeoylquinic acid, 3-caffeoylquinic acid, and scolymoside. The choleretic (bile stimulating) action of the plant has been well documented in a controlled trial involving a small sample of healthy volunteers.

6. Maitake Mushroom ext 20%: Maitake has a high content of polysaccharide compound called Beta Glucan, which stimulates the activities of immune cells. It also contains valuable nutrients such as vitamin C, D, B2, niacin, minerals (especially magnesium, potassium and calcium), fiber and amino acids, and yet it is extremely low in calories, fat, and cholesterol. The whole mushroom shows benefits as a tonic and is specifically useful in:

a. Lowering blood pressure
b. Reducing serum cholesterol
c. Lowering blood sugar
d. Weight loss
e. Constipation
f. Uterine fibroids
g. Stimulating cellular immunity

h.   Inhibiting tumor growth and metastasis

i.   Used during conventional cancer treatment to reduce side-effects such as hair loss, pain, fatigue and nausea

7. An isolated beta-glucan component, known as D-fraction, functions as a potent immune modulator by boosting the body's own immune responses including natural killer cells, cytotoxic T-cells, macrophage, super oxide anion cells and interleukin.

72.00 mg	Vitamin C (Ester C)
190.00 mg	Phosophatidyl Choline Complex
100.00 mg	Milk Thistle Seed Ext 80%
90.00 mg	Calcium D-glucarate
50.00 mg	Artichoke ext 2% Cynarin
50.00 mg	Maitake Mushroom ext 20%
290.00 mg	Proprietary Support Blend

***Schizandra Berry Ext 4:1 Shitake Mushroom Dandelion Root Bupleurum Root Shitake mushroom ext 4:1 Meitake Mushroom Reishi Mushroom ext 10:1 Dong quai Root Ext 4:1 Garlic Clove Ext 4:1 Lycil Fruit Ginger Root Wild Yam Root

For More Information See
The Following Web Sites

◊   http://www.health-pages.com/

◊   http://www.healthandage.com/

◊   http://www.doctorstrust.com/

◊   *http://www.vitacost.com/*

◊   http://www.shokos.com

Most Common Mental Health Disorders
Associated with Substance Abuse

BIPOLAR DISORDER: Also known as manic-depressive illness, it is a brain disorder that causes unusual and severe shifts in mood, energy, and ability to function. Different from the normal ups and downs that everyone goes through, the symptoms of bipolar disorder are severe. Bipolar disorder causes dramatic mood swings from overly "high" and/or irritable to sad and hopeless, and then back again, often with periods of normal mood in between. Severe changes in energy and behavior go along with these changes in mood. The periods of highs and lows are called episodes of mania and depression.

Signs and symptoms of mania (or a manic episode) include:

a.   Increased energy, activity, and restlessness
b.   Excessively "high," overly good, euphoric mood

c. Extreme irritability
d. Racing thoughts and talking very fast, jumping from one idea to another
e. Distractibility, can't concentrate well
    Little sleep needed
f. Unrealistic beliefs in one's abilities and powers
g. Poor judgment
h. Spending sprees
i. A lasting period of behavior that is different from usual
j. Increased sexual drive
k. Abuse of drugs, particularly cocaine, alcohol, and sleeping medications
1. Provocative, intrusive, or aggressive behavior
m. Denial that anything is wrong

Signs and symptoms of depression (or a depressive episode) include

a. Lasting sad, anxious, or empty mood
b. Feelings of hopelessness or pessimism
c. Feelings of guilt, worthlessness, or helplessness
d. Loss of interest or pleasure in activities once enjoyed, including sex
e. Decreased energy, a feeling of fatigue or of being "slowed down"

f.   Difficulty concentrating, remembering, making decisions

g.   Restlessness or irritability

h.   Sleeping too much, or can't sleep

i.   Change in appetite and/or unintended weight loss or gain

j.   Chronic pain or other persistent bodily symptoms that are not caused by physical illness or injury

k.   Thoughts of death or suicide, or suicide attempts

Source: www.nimh.nih.gov/publicat/bipolar.cfm

GENERALIZED ANXIETY DISORDER (GAD): Characterized by 6 or more months of persistent, exaggerated worry and tension that is unfounded or much more severe than the normal anxiety most people experience. People with these disorders usually expect the worst; they worry excessively about money, health, family, or work, even when there are no signs of trouble. They are unable to relax and often suffer from insomnia. Many people with GAD also have physical symptoms, such as fatigue, trembling, muscle tension, headaches, irritability, or hot flashes. GAD often coexists with depression, substance abuse, or other anxiety disorders. Other conditions associated with stress, such as irritable bowel syndrome, often accompany GAD.

Source: www.nimh.nih.gov/Publicat/gadfacts.cfm

PANIC DISORDER: Characterized by unexpected and repeated episodes of intense fear accompanied by physical symptoms that may include chest pain, heart palpitations, shortness of breath, dizziness or abdominal distress. These sensations often mimic symptoms of a heart attack or other life-threatening medical conditions. This disorder is often accompanied by phobias about places or situations. Research shows that panic disorder most often coexists with depression and substance abuse. About 30% of people with panic disorder abuse alcohol and 17% abuse drugs, such as cocaine and marijuana, in unsuccessful attempts to alleviate the anguish and distress caused by their condition.
Source: www.nimh.nih.gov/publicat/panicfacts.cfm

DEPRESSION: This is a serious medical illness; it's not something that has been made up in your head. It's feeling "down" and "low" and "hopeless" for weeks at a time, most often accompanies substance/ alcohol abuse.

Signs & Symptoms:

    a.   Persistent sad, anxious, or "empty" mood
    b.   Feelings of hopelessness, pessimism

c. Feelings of guilt, worthlessness, helplessness

d. Loss of interest or pleasure in hobbies and activities that were once enjoyed

Source: www.nihm.nih.gov/healthinformation/depressionmenu.cfm

ATTENTION DEFICIT HYPERACTIVITY DISORDER (AD-HD): It is one of the most common mental disorders that develop in children. Children with ADHD have impaired functioning in multiple settings, including home, school, and in relationships with peers. If untreated, the disorder can have long-term adverse effects into adolescence and adulthood such as higher rates of injury, depressive, anxiety, and conduct disorders, drug abuse, such as cocaine and methamphetamines, or antisocial behavior.

Signs & Symptoms:

a. Impulsiveness
b. Hyperactivity, restlessness, fidgety
c. Inattention, lack of focus
d. Losing things
e. Disorganized

Source: www.nimh.nih.gov/HealthInformation/adhdmenu.cfm

OBSESSIVE COMPULSIVE DISORDER (OCD): An anxiety disorder that is characterized by recurrent, unwanted thoughts (obsessions) and/or repetitive behaviors (compulsions). Repetitive behaviors such as hand washing, counting, checking, or cleaning are often performed with the hope of preventing obsessive thoughts or making them go away. Performing these so-called "rituals," however, provides only temporary relief, and not performing them markedly increases anxiety. Source: www.nimh.nig.gov/HealthInformation/ocd-menu.cfm

POST-TRAUMATIC STRESS DISORDER (PTSD): An anxiety disorder that can develop after exposure to a terrifying event or ordeal in which grave physical harm occurred or was threatened. Traumatic events that may trigger PTSD include violent personal assaults, natural or human-caused disasters, accidents, or military combat. People with PTSD have persistent frightening thoughts and memories of their ordeal and feel emotionally numb, especially with people they were once close to. They may experience sleep problems, feel detached or numb, or be easily startled. Feelings of intense guilt are also common. Co-occurring depression, alcohol, or other substance abuse, or another anxiety disorders are not uncommon. Source: www.nimh.nih.gov/publicat/ptsdfacts.cfm

Glossary

12 Steps: A guide to help alcoholics/addicts/gamblers and food addicts to acquire a new way of life

AA: Alcoholics Anonymous, a self-help group of recovering alcoholics

Al-Anon: A self help group for families of alcoholics

Dual Diagnoses: Person who has 2 different disorders coexisting (existing at the same time) such as substance abuse & mental health disorders

GA: Gamblers Anonymous, a self-help group for recovering gamblers

NA: Narcotics Anonymous, a self-help group of recovering drug addicts

Nar-Anon: A self help group for families of addicts

OA: Overeaters Anonymous, a self-help group for overeaters

Sponsor: A person who guides you through the 12 steps. A person you can learn to have a healthy relationship with. Not based on sex, but on trust, understanding, and communication. It's based on one addict helping another.

Relapse Prevention Questionnaire

This questionnaire will help you to assess your strengths and weaknesses. Please do your best to answer as objectively as possible. This will form the basis for your relapse prevention program and your treatment plan.

1. Do you go to AA, NA, or both?

2. How many meetings have you gone to in the last three months?

3. How many meetings have you gone to in the last two weeks?

4. Do you get angry about having to go to meetings?
Yes__ No__ Sometimes__
If yes, give an explanation:

5. Are you involved in any AA or NA service ?
        Yes __ No__ Sometimes__
6. Do you reach out at meetings to help any newcomers?
        Yes __ No__ Sometimes__
    If yes or sometimes, when was the last time you did so?

7. Do you share at meetings?
        Yes __ No__ Sometimes__
8. Out of the last ten meetings, how many times did you raise your hand and share? __
9. Do you leave your AA/NA meetings before they are finished?
        Yes__ No__ Sometimes__
    If yes or sometimes, reasons:

10. Do you go to meetings at least ten minutes early and stay until after they have finish?
        Yes__ No__ Sometimes__
11. Do you go to meetings and find yourself always looking around and not paying attention?
        Yes__ No__ Sometimes__
12. Are you bored at meetings?
        Yes__ No__ Sometimes__

13. Do you go to any AA or NA social events?

        Yes__ No__ Sometimes__

14. Have you done any 12 step work in the last three months?

        Yes__ No__ Sometimes__

15. Do you have a home group?

        Yes__ No__

If no, how come?

16. Do you go to meetings when you are not feeling emotionally well?

        Yes__ No__ Sometimes__

If no or sometimes, give brief explanation why you choose not to:

17. Do you slack off on attending your meetings because you're feeling good?

        Yes__ No__ Sometimes__

If yes or sometimes, give brief explanation why you choose not to:

18. Do you enjoy going to meetings?

        Yes__ No__ Sometimes__

If no or sometimes, give brief explanation of what you do not like:

19. Do you have a sponsor?

Yes__ No__

20. What action have you taken to get a sponsor? Give a brief explanation:

21. How long have you been free of all mood-altering substances? How many sponsors did you have in this period of time, if any?

What was the longest period of time you worked with one?

22. Do you feel comfortable with your current sponsor?

Yes__ No__ Sometimes__

If no or sometimes, give a brief explanation for you discomfort:

23. How often do you call your sponsor?

24. In the last two weeks how often have you called your sponsor?

25. Do you lie or tell half-truths to your sponsor?
                 Yes__ No__ Sometimes__
    If yes or sometimes, give brief explanation of what prevents you from being honest:

26. Does your sponsor encourage you to w o r k the Twelve Steps of Recovery?
                      Yes__ No__
27. Are you working on your Twelve Steps of Recovery?
                      Yes__ No__
28. What step are you on?

29. How long have you been working on this step?

30. Do you feel stuck on a particular step?
        Yes __ No__ Maybe__
    If yes or maybe, give a brief explanation:

31. What other steps are you having difficulty with, if any?

32. Are you seeking any help in working the steps?
        Yes__ No__
33. Is your sponsor helping you with your steps?
        Yes__ No__ Sometimes__

34. Does your sponsor encourage you to go to meetings?
        Yes__ No__ Sometimes__
35. How many meetings a week does your sponsor encourage you to attend?

36. Do you feel you can get over on your sponsor?
        Yes__ No__ Sometimes__
    If yes or sometimes, give a brief explanation

how that makes you feel about yourself and your sponsor:

37. Did you pick a sponsor that you felt would make you work on your recovery?
Yes __No__

38. Did you pick a sponsor that you felt would not be so hard on you and that you could manipulate?
Yes__ No__
If yes, give a brief explanation why you picked such a sponsor:

39. If you are not satisfied with your current sponsor, what steps have you taken to rectify this? Give a brief explanation:

40. How long have you known that you are dissatisfied with your sponsor?

41. How long has your sponsor been clean?

42. Do you sponsor anyone?

Yes __ No__

If yes, how many people?_____

43. Are you feeling overwhelmed or uncomfortable sponsoring these people?

Yes__ No__ Sometimes__

If yes or sometimes, give a brief explanation for your discomfort:

44. Are you sponsoring anyone of the opposite sex?

Yes__ No__ Sometimes__

If yes or sometimes, give a brief description of the circumstances and your reasoning:

45. Do you, as a sponsor, feel you are setting a good example of recovery?

Yes__ No__ Sometimes__

If no or maybe, give a brief explanation for the way you feel:

46. What do you need to change to become a better sponsor?

47. Give a brief explanation of what being a sponsor means to you and what you expect from a sponsor.

48. Do you drink coffee or tea with caffeine?
                Yes__ No__ Sometimes__
49. Do you drink espresso or Cuban coffee?
                Yes__ No__ Sometimes__
    If yes, give amounts you drink on a daily basis:

50 Do you drink soda with caffeine?
                Yes__ No__
    If yes, how many in an average day?

51. Do you eat chocolate or any products made with chocolate?
                Yes__ No__ Sometimes__
    If yes, how much and how often? Explain:

52. Do you use white sugar (refined sugar) or products that have white sugar in them? If yes, what kind, how often and how much on an average day?

53. Do you eat white flour products (bagels, white bread, cake, etc.)? If yes, what kind, how often and how much on an average day?

54. Do you find yourself craving sweets when you feel stressed or happy?

Yes__ No__ Sometimes__

55. Do you smoke cigarettes or any other form of Tobacco?

Yes__ No__

If yes, how much, how often and what kind of Tobacco? Also, include how long you have been smoking:

56. Do you eat past 7:00 p.m.?

Yes__ No__ Sometimes__

If yes or sometimes, how often in a week? Is it a heavy, medium or light meal? Also, describe each meal:

57. How long before you go to sleep do you eat? Explain:

58. Do you eat red meat?

Yes__No__

More than once a week?

Yes__No__

59. Do you eat three good meals a day?

Yes__ No__ Sometimes__

If no, how many meals do you eat in an average day and describe briefly what these meals consist of:

60. Do you take any vitamins or supplements?

Yes __ No__ Sometimes ___

If yes, what kind, how often and when are they taken?

When was the last time taken?

61. Have you ever been checked for hyper or hypoglycemia?

Yes__ No__

Last check up?

If you have it, what are you doing for it?

62. Do you have any other illnesses that you know of?

If yes, explain:

63. Do you exercise regularly?

Yes__ No__ Sometimes__

If yes or sometimes, describe what kind of exercise and how often you work out in a week.

Also, what average length of time you spend exercising, and when was the last time you worked out? If no, give reasons why you do not work out:

a. Do you sweat when you work out?

Yes__ No__ Sometimes__

b. What do you like or dislike about exercise?

c. Do you consider yourself overweight?

Yes__ No__

If yes, how many pounds do you feel you need to lose for you to feel comfortable?

d. If under weight, how many pounds do you feel you have to gain?

68. Do you consider yourself a compulsive eater?
Yes__ No__ Sometimes__

69. Do you eat in excess when you feel stressed?
Yes__ No__ Sometimes__
If yes or sometimes, give a brief explanation:

70. Do you overeat when you are feeling good?
Yes__ No__ Sometimes__
If yes or sometimes, give a brief explanation:

71. Do you overeat to get back at someone?
Yes__ No__ Sometimes__
If yes or sometimes, give a brief explanation:

72. Do you have a job or own your own business?
Yes__ No__

73. In an average week, how many hours per day do you work?

74. Do you bring work home?

Yes__ No__

If yes, how often:

75. Is your mind preoccupied with your job?

Always__ Sometimes__ Rarely__

76. Do you find yourself obsessing about making money?

Always__ Sometimes__ Rarely__

77. Are you happy with the work you are doing?

Yes__ No__ Sometimes__

If no or sometimes, give a brief explanation:

78. List alternatives you have in order to increase your work satisfaction:

79. Have you taken any action?

Yes__ No__

If yes, give a brief explanation of what action you took:

80. What kind of work would you like to do (work in sales, with your hands, etc.)?

81. What is preventing you from doing this?

82. Are you married?
                    Yes__ No__
    If yes, how long?
83. Are you in a relationship?
                    Yes__ No__
84. Briefly describe what you consider to be a healthy relationship:

85. Is your relationship monogamous?
                    Yes__ No__ Sometimes__
    If no or sometimes, explain last outside encounter and how you felt afterwards:

86. How many times in an average day do you find yourself looking at or daydreaming about people in a sexual way?

87. How much of your time do you feel is spent on these thoughts? Give approximate time?

88. Do you find the frequency increasing during times of stress?

Yes __ No__

During times of boredom?

Yes __ No__

When you are feeling good about yourself?

Yes __ No__

Give a brief explanation:

89. Do you feel you need a relationship in order to be complete?

Yes__ No__ Sometimes__

If yes or sometimes, give a brief explanation:

90. Do you masturbate?

Yes__ No__ Sometimes__

If yes, how often in an average week?

91. Do you find yourself masturbating more often during times of stress?

Yes__ No__

During times of boredom?

Yes__ No__

When you are feeling good about yourself?

Yes__ No__

Give a brief explanation:

92. Do you use sex to cover up or change your feelings?

Yes__ No__ Sometimes__

Give a brief explanation:

93. List what you enjoy doing for fun (fishing, tennis, etc.)?

94. When was the last time you did something for fun?

95. In the last thirty days, how often did you do something for fun?

96. What did you do for fun?

97. Were other people involved in this activity?

98. How often in the last thirty days did you have fun with other people?

99. How often in the last thirty days did you have fun doing things alone?

100. Do you prefer doing these activities alone or with others?

Give a brief explanation:

101. Do you believe in a Higher Power?
Yes__ No__

102. How often do you pray to your Higher Power?
Everyday__ Sometimes__ Rarely__
If sometimes or rarely, give a brief explanation for your infrequency:

103. Do you pray for your will?
Yes__ No__ Sometimes__
Give a brief explanation for your answer:

104. Do you feel a Higher Power can help you?
Yes__ No__

If yes, how do you expect your Higher Power to help you?

105. Do you pray to your Higher Power mostly when you are in trouble?
Yes__ No__

106. Do you pray to your Higher Power when things are going well?
Yes__ No__ Sometimes__
If yes or sometimes, give reason why:

107. Do you feel you need to get more in touch with a Higher Power?
Yes__ No__ Maybe__
Give a brief explanation for your answer:

108. Do you feel you practice humility when you pray?
Yes__ No__ Sometimes__
If no or sometimes, give brief explanation why you do not:

109. Do you concentrate and are you sincere when you pray, or do you just say the words so you can get it over with?

Yes__ No__ Sometimes__

If no or sometimes, describe reason and circumstances for your attitude:

110. Do you meditate or allow yourself some quiet time away from everyone and everything?

Yes__ No__ Sometimes__

If yes or sometimes, how often?

If no, give a brief explanation for not practicing:

111. How do you meditate or practice quiet time?

Give a brief explanation:

112. Are you a grateful recovering person?

Yes__ No__ Sometimes__

If yes or sometimes, explain why:

113.   Do you have trouble making friends?
        Yes__ No__ Sometimes__
    If yes or sometimes, explain why you think it
is hard for you: What action have you been taking
to change this?

114.   Do you find yourself feeling lonely (choose
from last experience)?
        Often__ Sometimes__ Hardly Ever__
    If you answered often or sometimes, describe
what action you took to address this feeling and
how it helped?

    If you took little or no action, explain, as best
you can why:

115.   Do you find yourself bored (choose from
last experience)?
        Often__ Sometimes__ Hardly Ever__
    If often or sometimes, describe what action was
taken to address this feeling and how it helped:

If little or no action was taken explain, as best you can, why:

116.   Do you find yourself feeling overwhelmed (choose from last experience)?
Often__ Sometimes__ Hardly Ever __
If you answered often or sometimes, describe what action you took to address this feeling and how it helped:

If no or very little action was taken, explain, as best you can, why:

117.   Do you gamble?
Yes__ No__ Sometimes__
If yes or sometimes, how often in an average thirty day period?

How much did you spend?
Could you afford to spend that much?

118.   Do you find yourself gambling more when you are?

Angry __ Bored __ Lonely__ Depressed__
Happy__Doesn't matter__

119.   Do you feel you are a compulsive gambler?

Yes__ No__ Sometimes__

Explain your answer briefly:

120.   Do you find yourself shopping for things you do not need?

Yes__ No__ Sometimes__

If yes or sometimes, briefly explain why:

121.   Do you find yourself shopping more when you are?

Angry__ Bored__ Lonely__ Depressed__ Happy__ Does not matter__

122.   Do you consider yourself a compulsive shopper?

Yes__ No__ Sometimes__

If yes or sometimes, briefly explain your answer:

IDENTIFIED PROBLEMS

_____
_____
_____
_____
_____
_____
_____
_____
_____
_____
_____
_____

SUMMARY/EVALUATION
OF YOUR RECOVERY

IMMEDIATE GOALS

Time frame when they will start and when they will be completed.

1. _____

_____

_____

_____

2. _____

_____

_____

_____

3. _____

_____

_____

_____

4. _____

_____

_____

_____

5. _____

_____

_____

----

6.   _____

LONG TERM GOALS

Give estimated beginning and completion dates

1.   _____

----

2.   _____

----

3.   _____

GO FOR IT!!!

Suggested Readings

Alcoholics Anonymous

Beyond Prozac: Brain-Toxic Lifestyles, Natural Antidotes and New Generation Antidepressants by Michael J Norden, MD

Codependent No More: How to Stop Controlling Others and Start Caring for Yourself, by Melody Beattie

Facing Love Addiction: Giving Yourself the Power to Change the Way You Love—The Love Connection to Codependence, by Pia Mellody

Gamblers Anonymous: A Day at a Time, by Anonymous

Hinds Feet on High Places, by Hannah Hurnard

It's Not Your Fault: Overcoming Anorexia and Bulimia Through Biopsychiatry, by Russell Marx, M.D.

Na Text: Narcotics Anonymous

Seven weeks to Sobriety, by Joan Mathews Larson Ph.D.

Sex and Love Addicts Anonymous, by Augustine Fellowship *Staff*

SHAMBHALA the Sacred Path of the Warrior, by Chogyam Trungpa, Carolyn Rose Gimian (Editor)

The Celestine Prophecy, by James Redfield

The Twelve Steps and Twelve Traditions of Overeaters

Anonymous, by Overeaters Anonymous Incorporated

Way of the Peaceful Warrior, by Dan Millman

Some of the excerpts that are in this book are taken from the books that are in the suggested readings.

Telephone Numbers
AA/NA

◊ AL-ANON Family Headquarters: 757–563–1600

◊ Rational Recovery: 916–621–2667

◊ National number for AA: 212–647–1680

◊ National number for NA: 818–773–9999

◊ Addictions

◊ Co-dependents Anonymous: 602–277–7991

◊ Debtors Anonymous: 212–642–8220

◊ Gamblers Anonymous Hotline: 800–397–9843

◊ National Cocaine Hotline: 800–262–2463

◊ Overeaters Anonymous: 505–891–2664

◊ AIDS Hotline: 1–800–342–2437

◊ Spanish AIDS Hotline: 1–800–344–7432

Our Vision

Giordano & Goldfarb's Holistic Addiction Treatment Program is dedicated to improving treatment outcomes. We investigate new treatment modalities that have the potential to improve treatment outcomes. We are not afraid to think out of the box, especially when someone's life is at stake. Our centers have been designed for those souls who are tormented by their addictions and associated behaviors. The strategies we use are for successful continuous recovery from addictive disorders. Some of our information, methods, treatment, and suggestions are from medical doctors, addictionologists, and psychiatrists. Additional gathered information comes from recovering addicts who were once among the living dead and now share a bond with their Higher Power. Maintaining continuous recovery is our goal. Our 1st priority is a commitment to those who commit to themselves. May God continue to guide us.

Respectfully,
John Giordano, C.A.P.

1-800-559-9503

TATE PUBLISHING & *Enterprises*

Tate Publishing is commited to excellence in the publishing industry. Our staff of highly trained professionals, including editors, graphic designers, and marketing personnel, work together to produce the very finest books available. The company reflects the philosophy established by the founders, based on Psalms 68:11,

"THE LORD GAVE THE WORD AND GREAT WAS THE COMPANY OF THOSE WHO PUBLISHED IT."

If you would like further information, please call
1.888.361.9473
or visit our website
www.tatepublishing.com

TATE PUBLISHING & *Enterprises*, LLC
127 E. Trade Center Terrace
Mustang, Oklahoma 73064 USA